SOFTBALL IN
THE VILLAGES® COMMUNITY

'Senior Softball Heaven'

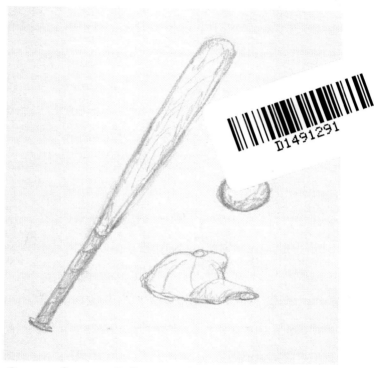

An Overview of the Softball Program, Opportunities, Facilities, Players and Volunteers Who Make This All Possible

By DAN KINCAID

Copyright© 2020 by Dan Kincaid

ISBN 9798665042190

Published by: Kade Holley Publishing

Editing: Kade Holley, Shannon Lough

Cover Design: Kade Holley, Shannon Lough

Cover Photo: Dan Kincaid

Interior Title Page Sketch: Mary Linscheid

Interior Photos: Dan Kincaid (or others where noted)

Special thanks to Avis Vaught for her contributions to this publication. Others noted throughout the book.

The Villages® is a registered trademark of Holding Company of The Villages, Inc. This book is not affiliated with, or sponsored by, Holding Company of the Villages, Inc. or its affiliated entities.

Printed in the United States of America

**Typical Men's Softball Team –
The "Barracudas" –In the Winter 2020 season-
68+ League at Soaring Eagle fields**

**(L-R) Back row: Bob Seeber, Dave Williams,
Paul Hoecker, Dan Kincaid, Bob Henry, Bob
Alan.**

**(L-R) Front row: Guy Pellier (sub), Lou Daigle,
Dana Lambillotte (Manager), Floyd Davis.**

**Absent: Steve Kurkui, Chuck Novet, Ricky
Pellino**

Photo courtesy of Al Wolter (2020)

**Typical Women's Softball Team –
The "Four Corners" - Ladies Rec 2 –Fall 2018
season at the Buffalo Glen fields**

**(L-R): Patty Boley, Avis Vaught, Nora Kimble,
Peggy Coulture, Donna Levery, Erica Bowler,
Karon Stockman, Jackie Fritts, Cindy Flannery,
Sis Dueholm, Dinah Heidebrink**

Photo courtesy of Avis Vaught (2018)

REVIEWS AND READER COMMENTS

Softball in The Villages® community has grown from a small group of men and women practicing and playing pickup games at the Knudson Field to what it is today – a major part of the overall recreation programs that we have to offer. We now have 15 beautiful, well maintained fields on which to play softball. The Recreation and Neighborhood Leagues have seen phenomenal growth. In addition, we have various other leagues, as well as travel and tournament teams involved with softball here. Last year alone, counting all of these various opportunities, there were nearly 3,000 players, participating on over 200 teams in our community. Dan Kincaid's book provides a glimpse into our softball history here, as well as an overview of where things stand today. I think you will find the player Bio's and interviews especially interesting.

Pam Henry - Recreation Manager - Lifestyle, Parks, and Public Relations.

Dan's book will be very helpful for newcomers who want to learn about softball opportunities in The Villages® community. Long-time residents and current softball players will also, I'm sure, find the information in this book very interesting.

Vernon Brooks – Long-time manager and player in the Recreation and Neighborhood Leagues, as well as the Central Florida League (CFL).

I think this book is a very good overview of the local softball scene. New residents and veteran players alike will find it informative. The player interviews and Bio's are extremely interesting. Dan made sure he covered both the women's programs and the men's programs in his book.

Avis L. Vaught – Avis has served on the Softball Advisory Board and the Ladies Rec 1 Board. She currently serves on the Softball Evaluation Committee and helps conduct skills clinics for the women. Avis has been a long-time player, manager, umpire, and scorekeeper for women's softball.

When I arrived in The Villages® community in 1998, the entire softball program consisted of two divisions, playing all their games at Knudson Field. In fact, in the summers we only had enough players for one division. With over 3,000 players now, I can imagine that new residents could be easily overwhelmed by the sheer numbers and the inherent complexity resulting from such growth. For them, what Dan Kincaid has compiled will be an excellent introduction for anyone looking to participate in this sport. In addition, Dan is also providing historical and biographical notes that will be of interest to anyone already involved with softball here.

Joe Sanchez – President of the original Villages Softball Association; over 20 years as a player, manager, statistician, and umpire at every level of the Recreation Leagues, as well as the Restricted Bat League (RBL), 68+ League, and the Neighborhood Leagues.

TABLE OF CONTENTS

Dedication   vii

I. Preface and Acknowledgements   1

II. Introduction/General Overview   9

III. Primary Leagues and Divisions   43

IV. Other Leagues and Teams   69

V. Appendix - Player Bio's: 91
   -   Men's   96
   -   Women's   227

VI. Postscript   251

Photos   254

References   273

Other Books by Dan Kincaid   275

Author Bio   277

DEDICATION

This book is dedicated to all of the current, past, and future individuals and organizations responsible for making softball in The Villages® community such a wonderful and enjoyable experience for everyone.

This includes: the administrators; league officers and board members; players, coaches, managers, umpires, and scorekeepers; those who prepare and maintain the fields; those who maintain websites and statistical records; sponsors; concession operators; spectators; and various other officials and volunteers who make these programs function at such a high level.

Many folks who have been instrumental in the softball community here have passed on and we are forever grateful to them for their contributions. Two of those people were extremely helpful to me. A special recognition to: **Fran Nencetti** and **Dan List**.

Fran helped me throughout my evaluation process and my playing days in the Neighborhood League. I talked with him numerous times and he was always very helpful and encouraging. He even called me once to tell me that he had found my glove, which I had left at Buffalo Glen ....something he predicted would happen.

I got to know Dan at some open field practices and then in both the Recreation and RBL Leagues. One year when I moved up to play in Division 2, Dan drafted me to play for his Marlins team and it was a great experience. He was certainly an inspiration to me, as he was to many others.

I. PREFACE AND ACKNOWLEDGEMENTS

I'm not sure how many times someone has mentioned to me that **'they'** should write a book about softball in The Villages® community; but it has been numerous times. And knowing that I have written several books, some friends suggested that I do it. Well, I guess I'm the **'they'** that finally writes the book.

Up front, you should understand that this is merely an overview of softball here, not a comprehensive or in-depth coverage. For that reason, I think the primary audience for this book will be the new resident wanting to find out more about local softball opportunities; or perhaps even longer term residents who want to know more about the subject before beginning to play.

But veteran softball players will also be especially interested in the Appendix listing of player Bio's, where I have tried to provide a representative cross-section of men and women from every league and every division – what leagues do they play in; where did they move here from; what are their sports and softball backgrounds; general comments on softball here; and so on. There are over 125 individual player profiles in the Appendix.

I'll be sure to mention it a couple of more times later in the book....... that there are so many different aspects of playing softball here that you simply cannot cover it all. Rules that are specific to one league may not be to another; plus rules vary from year to year and season to season in many leagues.

With over 20 various leagues, including both men's and women's, the travel teams, recreation leagues, age groups, neighborhood leagues, and several specialty leagues and teams, I think you can see the dilemma. It's definitely a case of 'one size does not fit all.' But that's a good thing because there is definitely something here for everyone.

What I write today may not hold true next year. For that reason, I'll try not to dive too deeply into the various rules. Still, I want to provide the reader with some idea of the differences in the leagues, skill levels, etc. But please, just use this as an introductory guide and not the gospel on every detail.

I may have gotten something wrong within these pages or it may have changed by the time you read this, but I've tried to be as accurate and thorough as possible. Just use this as an introductory glimpse into softball here and once you get involved, the managers and other experienced players, coaches, and administrators will keep you straight on the various rules and regulations.

 And remember that no matter what the specific rules may be, it is still basically just softball; nothing more.

This also reminds me of something else: the spelling or, should I say, the mis-spelling of names. I'm fairly sure that I have the names spelled correctly that are featured in the Appendix of Player Bio's. But when I interviewed people about the various names of other individuals who helped start leagues or who were important in some of the leagues, I got a lot of "I can't remember how he or she spelled their name" or "I forget his last name" or "I think it was something like ......?" So bear with me on that particular matter. As we all age (me included), it's definitely more difficult to remember some of these details.

I tried to check out spellings as much as I could, but forgive me if I have spelled your name or one of your friend's names wrong. My last name is spelled 'Kincaid' but in the past few years I have seen it spelled in print as Kincade, Kinkade, Kinkaid, and even once as Cinkade. So, I feel your pain if I have misspelled your name, but please, please give me some slack on that.

As far as mentioning players and others who have been or are currently instrumental in softball here, there are those 125+ people featured in the Appendix Bio's. But it would be nearly impossible to mention everyone who is involved in the sport locally, much less those who have been involved over the past 25+ years. That number would range in the many thousands.

I recently read that over 2,800 people played softball here during the 2019 year, playing in those 20+ leagues on more than 200 teams. And I guess those numbers are even greater, if you try to accurately include all of the travel teams. So, the players mentioned in this book are just meant to provide **a small representative cross-section** from all of the leagues and genders, all divisions; and some of the more recent players, as well as long-time players, etc.

I also read a few weeks ago that the population of The Villages® community 22 years ago was about 14,000. Now in 2020 it is around 130,000. With that increase in population, of course, there has been an almost exponential growth of the interest in softball. It has become somewhat complicated to keep it all going smoothly, but somehow it does, primarily because of the expertise of the Recreation staff; and the various league officers, managers, and volunteers. With 15 fields now to play on, it is truly a hotbed for senior softball in the United States.

In any case, this book should provide newcomers with an idea of what softball is all about in the community. And hopefully it is also a 'shout out' to many players and others who make this all work. And I do apologize, again, if I have left out mentioning someone who you think should have been included. There are just so many!

I had heard about senior softball in Florida and I even saw a segment about it on television 10 or 15 years ago. It was intriguing, but I never thought I would be involved. After all, I never planned to retire in Florida; being a forest ranger from the hardwood country of the Appalachian Mountains, Florida was never my cup of tea, so to speak. I just like mountains and trees, I guess. Plus, I had not played softball for 25 years. However, things changed for me around 2010.

I developed a health condition that doctors kept telling me necessitated a move to a warmer climate, especially during the cooler months up north. I won't go into too many details; after all, that is not what this book is about. The 'short story' is that I begin to lose red blood cells when I'm exposed to temperatures below the mid-60 degree range. And that's not a good thing. Of course, it's a little more complicated than that and it involves clotting, among other things.

After dragging my feet on the doctor recommendations, and after having some very low test results for red blood cell count and hemoglobin, my wife insisted we pack up for the winter months and head to Florida. My wife is a registered nurse and she can be very persuasive, shall we say. That was in 2013.

We visited a few friends and locations down here and I was again convinced that Florida was not where I wanted to live, at least not full-time. We're not beach people and again, being a forester, I knew I would miss the mountains and the trees. Way too many palms here.

But Vicki had read about The Villages® community online and decided that we should do one of the 'lifestyle previews.' **Stop me if you've heard this one before!** – We visited and almost immediately we were hooked.

What happened was that one day we had stopped by the Saddlebrook softball fields. I walked up to the outfield fence and just stood there in awe. The fields and facilities were great and there were a bunch of older men out there playing softball! To paraphrase a comment that Ron Goldman makes in the Player Bio section of this book, I thought 'is this heaven?' And the answer was, 'no, this is The Villages.' Ron's paraphrase, of course, is based on a comment made in the baseball movie, Field of Dreams.

I don't know what division or league was playing at Saddlebrook that day, but it certainly seemed like I would be able to compete at that level. My wife said I looked like a little kid again, with a gleam in my eye, wanting to play ball. I strongly deny the part about looking like a little kid again, but that's my wife's story and she says she's sticking to it. But I did want to play ball again; I don't deny that.

Long story short, a few months later we bought a house here. For a year, we tried having a home in Ohio and one in Florida, but, for us, that was too much hassle. So, we sold our Athens, Ohio house and became year-round residents of The Villages® community.

Now, I'm not crazy about some of the extremely hot summer days here; and did I mention that I like mountains and trees? But with no snow and plenty of softball – about 9 ½ months of softball leagues each year, divided up into three separate seasons – I somehow make it work. And my wife has plenty to do with the various clubs and organizations. And there is the entertainment, the restaurants, the new friendships with people our own age, riding around in golf carts, and all of the activities. Did I mention it doesn't snow here and there is plenty of softball to be played? And, of course, for the most part my health condition has stayed under control here, too.

That's a little bit of the back story of why we're here. And obviously, I enjoy the softball scene so much that I am now writing this book about it.

Now let me quickly acknowledge a few people who have helped me gather information and who are heavily involved with softball here. Others will be mentioned in various chapters and in the Player Bio section of the book. After all, in addition to the great facilities and organization, it's the people who make this all work.

Of course, there needs to be an initial 'shout-out' to Mr. Harold Schwartz and his son Gary Morse who came up with the idea of The Villages® community and who grew the idea into this amazing place. Sadly, those two gentlemen have passed on, but the Morse family, along with their team of administrators and managers, has continued to lead the community through an unbelievable period of growth.

As for the overall amenities and the recreation opportunities, I would hardly know where to begin. But in softball itself, the leadership of John Rohan and Pam Henry has been extraordinary. John began his tenure here around 1993 and Pam in 1996. They have both been involved with softball as it grew from a few people practicing and playing 'pick-up' games on one field to where we are today.

Currently, the day-to-day softball program is being led by Danny Jacobs and Andrew Esposito, but both Rohan and Henry are still around, giving advice and providing overall guidance, as necessary. I've had several opportunities to talk with all four of these folks over the past several years and they are always willing to sit down and discuss anything in regard to the softball programs. I'm also told that Joe Bouthillette, Jack

Ware, and Travis Rima were very involved with the softball programs in previous years.

Those who have helped me gather information include: Pam Henry, Danny Jacobs, Andrew Esposito, Avis Vaught, Tom McGann, Jack Nesci, John Raines, Jack Nagle, Bill and Jeri Taylor, Matt Spanier, Dick Kanyan, Jack Kleffman, Billy Layton, Terry Cole, Doug White, Dave Mamuscia, Pam Napoletano, Frenchie Le Tan, Ted Ramirez, Bob Hrabak, Vernon Brooks, Judy Wanko, Wally Dias, Jane Girotti, Dave Bigelow, Jan Washburn, Joe Rocco, Ron Lottes, Bob Baker, Karen Coll, Joe Sanchez, Bob Nyce, Wayne Lockman, Darlene Hedrick, Wayne Meyer, Bill DiCarlo, Cathy Norris, and Charlie Monton. When you start listing names, you invariably leave someone out. I apologize if that has been the case.

A final note - I've tried to include in the Appendix Bio's at least five players from each and every league and division – men and women. A few people listed no longer play, but most do. And, of course, many of these players participate in multiple leagues.

Now, read on for a general overview of softball here, followed by some specific information about the various teams, leagues, and divisions.

II. INTRODUCTION/GENERAL OVERVIEW

Let me touch on a variety of topics in this section. It is a kind of mish-mash of things that may be helpful for a newcomer to at least be aware of. I can't begin to go into details about all of the specific rules for each league, but I'll try to cover the basics.

Before I forget it, and in case I don't mention it elsewhere in this book, there are a number of times that the fields are open for practices or for people to just go out and play some pick-up softball – toss the ball around, take batting practice, and so on. These open field times are listed in the weekly recreation news. Generally, these times are in the afternoons and evenings, but sometimes earlier in the day.

Also, unless there is a weekend tournament scheduled, the fields are usually open on Sundays. Check the weekly news or ask around. Often a group of players regularly meets at certain times and locations for open play. The first year or two that I was here, I attended some of those in order to get in a little extra practice. That was where I first met Jack Nagle and Dan List, among others.

As alluded to previously, you will no doubt find out as you become a softball player here, that the rules and guidelines vary between leagues, and may even change from season to season or year to year. It's actually difficult to keep track of. So, don't worry too much about that. You'll figure it out once the season begins, depending upon which league or leagues you are playing in. Your manager and the other players will help you keep track of things. And remember, as I have said elsewhere in the book, it's still, basically, just softball.

Rest assured that most things are normal: three outs per team each inning; four balls is a walk; three strikes (including if you hit a foul ball on the 3rd strike) and you're out; base running etiquette applies; you can tag up and advance on fly balls; the games are seven innings long; there are, generally, four outfielders plus a short fielder; and on and on and on; probably very similar to the way games are played where you're moving here from.

When new rules are instituted or changes are made for the next season, your manager will explain things to you well in advance. I'll mention a few of the specific rules later in the book, but I can't begin to cover them all.

Also, maybe this is a good place to mention that everyone who plays softball in The Villages® community (or really, if you participate in just about anything) must sign a 'release agreement' before you are allowed to participate. Bob Nyce tells me that when you go through softball evaluations, which are discussed later in this chapter, you will be asked to sign a release form there.

You will also be asked to show your resident ID card, or lessee-issued ID card, along with a photo ID, in order to participate in the evaluation process. Guests (and therefore guest passes) are not eligible to participate in evaluations (more on evaluations below.) However, guests are allowed to attend any of the 'open field' sessions where players get together for just a little batting practice or perhaps a fun pick-up game. Just bring your guest pass with you for that. But essentially, guests are not allowed to play in the official organized recreation or neighborhood softball leagues.

Also, a quick reminder – The Villages® Recreation Department sets the rules for participating in evaluations and softball play, as well as field and league scheduling.

Fields

The 15 fields all consist of standard softball layouts for foul lines, back stops, dugouts, coach's boxes, on deck circles, base locations, and so forth.

The fields are located at: Knudson, not far from the Paradise Recreation Center; Saddlebrook, near the Polo Fields and adjacent to the Saddlebrook Recreation Center; Buffalo Glen, near The Villages Charter School complex; Soaring Eagle, just across the road from the Rohan Regional Recreation Center and adjacent to the Soaring Eagle Air Gun Range; and Everglades, adjacent to the Everglades Regional Recreation Center.

Knudson, the original Villages softball field, was first open for play in 1984. It has one softball field.

Saddlebrook opened for play in October of 2000 and consists of four fields.

The Buffalo Glen complex was completed and opened in October of 2007. It also comprises four fields.

Soaring Eagle opened with a dedication game in January 2015. I was fortunate to be able to play in that game along with several of the players from Vernon Brooks' Dolphins team, the Rec 3 champions from the previous season. We played against a team comprised of staff members from The Villages® Recreation Department. As I recall, both John Rohan and Danny Jacobs played on that team. It was a fun game and I think we 'oldtimers' actually won. But who was keeping score! Soaring Eagle has two softball fields.

The four Everglades fields opened in November 2019.

Fences at Everglades, Soaring Eagle, Buffalo Glen, and Saddlebrook are 300 feet from home plate. The Knudson Field fence is 228 feet from home plate.

AUTHOR'S NOTE: (The Arena League fence is 250 feet from home plate. The Arena League plays off-site at Sacks Field just north of Rt. 466 off Rolling Acres Road and is managed by the Lady Lakes Recreation Department. This league is mentioned here and in a later chapter, because it consists mostly of Village players.)

There is a standard foul pole marker located on all fences down the right and left field lines.

The outfields are grass with the last 15 feet before the fence being dirt and designated as a warning track. The Knudson Field warning track is 10 feet wide. The infields are dirt.

Scoreboards are generally located just beyond the outfield fence in center field. These are nice electronic scoreboards that have large enough displays to be seen from the dugouts and the stands.

The tower locations are set back behind the home plate screens and are mostly on the second floor level so that scorekeepers and announcers can easily view the proceedings on the fields.

The towers are enclosed. Those at Saddlebrook, Buffalo Glen, and Everglades are situated in the center of where the action can be seen on all four fields. There are separate scorekeepers and announcers for each of the four games. The Soaring Eagle tower can view both of those fields, while the Knudson scorer's area is situated in an enclosed booth to easily view the action from behind the backstop on that lone field.

Abbreviations

Let me list most of the abbreviations you will see in this book. Sometimes I abbreviated to save space; other times to eliminate so many repetitive words. Most of these abbreviations are common to softball or baseball, while some are perhaps specific only to this area.

For the positions I use: P - pitcher; C – catcher; 1B – first base; 2B – second base; 3B – third base; SS – shortstop; SF – short field (sometimes players here also refer to this position as midfield or middle infielder); LF – left field; LCF – left center field; RCF – right center field; RF – right field. Some of the players in their Bio's in the Appendix have listed that they play IF

– infield, or OF – outfield. Sometimes I use 'ump' for umpire; 'mgr' for manager; and 'Bd member' for Board of Directors member, but I'm sure these abbreviations are commonly understood.

As for the leagues and divisions, R or Rec stands for the Recreation Leagues; D stands for Division (there are generally five divisions or levels of players for the men and three for the ladies, as explained below in the evaluations section); and N represents the Neighborhood Leagues. These will be addressed further later on in the book, as will these leagues: CFL (Central Florida League); RBL (Restricted Bat League); 68+ (Age 68 and older league); the Classics League; and the Arena League. If you see a capital 'L' it will refer to the ladies leagues and K will refer to the Knudson softball field. More on all of these later in the book, plus a brief mention of travel (tournament) teams, the Senior Games, and the annual Veterans Tournaments, but those are the basic abbreviations you will see in this book.

Evaluations

As you can imagine, with over 20 various softball leagues, and with players ranging in age from 40 (for women) and 50 (for men) all the way into their 80s, and yes, a few even into their 90s, the skill levels vary widely.

Some individuals have played baseball or softball continuously from their teens or twenties all the way to the present. Others played ball in their 20s or 30s, but gave it up, only to get back into it once moving here 25 or 30 years later; while others never really played much at all or maybe once or twice a year at a church picnic or family reunion. Then, also, there are the various injuries and age-related health issues that affect one's skill level.

And, in general, most of the players in their 40s or 50s run faster, hit the ball harder and farther, and throw better than those in, say, their 70s. There are definitely some exceptions to this: you will find it hard to believe how good some of these age 70+ players are; and, of course, a few of the 50-somethings, who haven't played much ball in their lives, tend to have lower skill levels.

The point is this: since skill levels vary widely it is important to match players as closely as possible to others with similar skills. That's a safety consideration and it also improves the level of competition. Believe me, once you've seen some of these folks playing, if you haven't played much at all or maybe even for 20 or 30 years, you will quickly see that a mismatch of skills could cause injuries or create other safety problems.

This all leads to the evaluation process. I recently talked about these things with Bob Nyce, who currently serves as the Lead Evaluator for softball here.

You will often hear potential players or newcomers say that they "heard you have to 'try out' in order to play softball. And many people don't want to think they have to 'try out' for a team at this age. Well, let's clear that up right off the bat. There are no tryouts. Everyone qualifies to play at some level.

Instead of tryouts, there are evaluations, held one morning a week, traditionally on Tuesday mornings at Buffalo Glen. You have to attend three of these evaluations, after which you will be placed in a division commensurate with your skill level. This is determined by a group of seasoned evaluators who will watch you throw, field, bat, and run. The men will be rated as a Division 1 through 5 player and then become eligible to play on a team in that respective division. One is the highest skill level and five is the lowest. Ladies Divisions are 1 through 3 with one being the highest skill level.

After participating for one season in a certain division, you may elect to move up or move down one level. That is important because some players improve their skill levels after a season or two and are easily able to move up a level; others find that after competing for a season or two at a certain level that they may be more competitive and more equal to other players if they move down a level. Other players stay with the level in which they were initially evaluated and play in the same league for many years.

It has all been thoroughly thought out and time tested and, in general, it seems to work very well. You always hear a few complaints about what level someone was evaluated at, but in most instances it all works out in the end; especially with the ability to move up or down a level the following season.

Bob Nyce supplied me with this list of people who assist with the softball evaluation process, current as of the spring 2020 season:

Day 1 Evaluators – <u>Men</u> – George Beize; Wendell Couch; Jack Kleffman; Ron Robson; Bob Schaible; Will Statom; Mike Heck. <u>Women</u> – Nanci Osborne; Avis Vaught.

Day 2 Evaluators – <u>Men</u> – Rich Voigt; Jerry Boetther; Ken Link; Mike Jeffries; Vern Benson; Bob Mitchell. <u>Women</u> – Jeannette (Jay) Nemoda; Judy Wanko.

Day 3 Evaluators – <u>Men</u> – Tom Gvist; Hank Culley; Billy Warble; Doug Aikey; Doug Goslee; David Sellars; John Raines. <u>Women</u> – Cindy Flannery; Helen Wesolowski.

I believe that most of the men try to be at the evaluations for all three days. Maybe there are some exceptions to this from time to time.

Avis Vaught told me that she and the other lady evaluators try to attend each week, also; and that they will generally take the women who are getting evaluated to a separate field for their evaluations. In the early years of the women's program, Midge Ferraro and Avis Vaught designed and helped establish certain evaluation criteria for the ladies. Avis and Midge had experience playing and coaching at the high school and college levels, as well as in numerous recreation leagues over the years.

In any case newcomers, both men and women, will be evaluated by people who are experienced and who work their hardest to place players in their proper divisions.

Hats off to Bob Nyce and his entire evaluation team. This is an important and a time consuming job. Thanks to everyone who is involved!

Season lengths and Drafts

One of the beauties of softball in Florida is that you can play year-round. In general, here in this community there are three separate league seasons: One is roughly January through March; the next is May – July; and the last one is approximately September through November. Now, these are just approximations; the actual seasons can vary a week or two on either end of those months. But you'll get a schedule before your season begins listing the dates, times, and fields on which you play.

The approximate month between seasons is to allow time to do any repair work or modifications to the fields or the facilities. And to give some of us time to heal! It all works out very well.

Travel and tourney teams will, obviously, have different schedules. Most of them play on weekends all year long, primarily in central and southern Florida, but fairly often they travel to other states to compete, too.

About two months before a league season begins, you can fill out a form to be considered for the next season's draft. These forms are available at one of the Recreation Centers; normally it has been at Saddlebrook. You just fill out the form for the league you want to play in and leave it in a box in the lobby. If you're currently on a team and wish to remain in that league for the next season, your manager will generally have a sheet available at one of your games for you to sign up.

Another well thought out feature of the softball program here is that there are 'drafts' of players before each season. That way, new teams are always formed. It's a great way to meet new people and make new friends. It also keeps one team from getting all the good players and keeping them from season to season. It levels out the competitive playing field, so to speak.

Players in a draft are generally rated as A, B, or C players; or sometimes as 1, 2, or 3 level players within a specific division or league based upon known or expected playing abilities. During the drafts the managers will try to even out the number of players from each level for every team. Don't confuse this with being evaluated as a Division 1-5 player (or Division 1-3 for the women.) It is a separate thing. As a player, you won't have to do anything; the various Boards and managers will take care of this. It's just a way to try to keep the competition levels as even as possible.

In some of the leagues, teams used to be able to 'protect' a set number of players, usually two or three, or maybe as many as five, and keep them on their team from year to year. But that has caused some problems and I think most leagues now have complete roster drafts for new teams each season. There may be one or two exceptions to this, and the travel teams have different roster considerations that they must follow. It's another thing you will become more familiar with as you get involved in the local softball scene.

Bats

There are, indeed, a few different kinds of bats in use here, depending upon which leagues you are playing in. That was all kind of new to me since I had not played softball for 25 years or more. And the last leagues in which I played in Ohio and West Virginia all used the old single wall aluminum bats. At that time a few of the oldtimers even still used wooden bats. Not anymore!

Now there are the newer 'composite' bats and the ball just seems to jump off of those bats – harder, faster, and further. But there are a few leagues, namely the Neighborhood Leagues that still use the older bats. Plus, certain leagues, such as the RBL, the Arena League, and the league at Knudson, use bats that some people say are half way between the newer and the older types of bats. The combined Neighborhood 1/2 League has also gone to those type of bats. N3, N4, and N5 still use single wall aluminum bats.

Most all of the players have their own bats, except those that are furnished in the N3, N4, and N5 Leagues, so I had to get a bat or bats when I started playing. They are not inexpensive. But to be honest, when you see the prices that golfers are paying for their newer clubs, it isn't all that much different. In fact, you'll likely have much less money tied up in softball bats than you will in golf clubs.

A couple of people I met early on in my softball days here helped get me started on bats. I was able to initially buy one used bat fairly cheaply that lasted almost two years. When it finally cracked, during a game, a teammate actually gave me one of his bats (he said, "I have five; you can just have this one.") A different player saw that bat a season later, liked it, and traded me two of his bats for that one. Seemed like a good deal to me. About a year later another player I had become friends with traded me an almost brand new bat for the two that I had.......and I'm still using it. And then, in the RBL modified bat league, a player who was moving back north sold me his bat for about half of what he had paid for it.

I've been pretty lucky in that regard, but if you talk around and let people know you're looking for a bat, you can generally find one at a decent price. I will tell you that Larry Rivellese, Vernon Brooks, Phil Palma, and Ray Saberg were very helpful to me in my early search for bats. And the one season that I was fortunate to play with Hank Culley in the combined D1/D2 summer league, he checked my bats and gave me some very helpful tips. There are also many other players who will help you out and give you advice. One thing you will soon find out in the softball community here is that practically everyone will help you in any way they can.

John Raines has played in Recreation Divisions 2, 3, and 4, the Neighborhood leagues, and the 68+ league. He is very knowledgeable about softball bats. We recently talked and he provided me with much of the following information that a newcomer will find useful.

There are several companies that manufacture bats and there are several different types and styles. Players have their favorites, of course, but most all of the brands are very good. Talk to some of the veteran players and you will begin to get an idea of which bat or bats may be most suited to you.

Most of the players in the recreation leagues and other competitive leagues use the senior softball bats that are rated 1.21 BPF and are full composite bats. The exceptions, as noted previously, are the neighborhood leagues, the RBL, and the Knudson K5 league, where the league rule states that only 1.20 BPF bats approved by ASA are legal. I'm not sure I fully understand the BPF ratings, nor do most of the players, I've learned. But it stands for Bat Performance Factor. It has to do with how lively the ball comes off the bat. And believe me, the ball comes off these composite bats very fast; much faster than I ever remember in the old days.

For the full composite 1.21 bats, John said that the ball can rebound off the bat at well over 100 mph. I have even heard of speeds of 120 mph or greater for elite players. Of course, some of this depends upon the individual batter, and how much bat speed he or she can generate with their swing. And most of this originates with lower arm and wrist strength, as opposed to upper body muscles.

I was watching some tournament games here a couple of years ago and a skinny guy from a south Florida team hit several balls over the fence. He was about 5' 9" tall and probably didn't weigh over 165 pounds. But he generated a ton of bat speed. Many of the taller, heavier, and stronger players did not hit any home runs. Of course, if you happen to be 6'3" tall, weigh 220 pounds, and have strong wrists, then that's even better. But again, upper body strength in itself is not the key.

Back to the bats. The RBL bats are generally one-piece or two-piece bats rated 1.20 BPF. John told me that rebound speeds for those bats are probably in the 80 mph range. That's still pretty darn fast. All of these various bat rebound speeds in today's softball make protective equipment very desirable and I will briefly discuss that later.

Most of the two-piece RBL bats have a composite handle and a single-wall aluminum or steel barrel. I currently use a two-piece, BPF 1.20, DeMarini single-wall steel bat with a 2 ¼ inch barrel and a composite handle. It's 34" long and weighs 26 ounces. The RBL league maintains a list of which bats are approved for use there, but the key is that they must be single-wall barrels. Wooden bats are actually all right to use, but you rarely see that any longer. I did see one person use a wooden bat when I first started playing in the RBL.

Andrew Esposito of the Recreation Department recently told me that the neighborhood leagues use 1.20 BPF, one-piece, single wall, Easton aluminum bats. The bats are furnished by the league for Divisions 3, 4, and 5. You don't bring your own. And having played in that league for several seasons, it is easy to tell that the bat rebound speeds are very low compared to the recreation leagues. The neighborhood bats seem to be more like those we used 30 years ago, although I'm sure they are much improved over those days. As mentioned previously, the Division 1/2 neighborhood league players are now allowed to use their own bats and they can be two-piece, similar to the RBL, as long as the compression ratio is 1.20 BPF.

Raines told me that the composite senior softball bats are pretty much all 34" in length with a 2 ¼ inch diameter barrel. They range in weight from 25 to 30 ounces with the most common probably being a 34" 27-ounce bat for the men. (I use a 34" 26-ounce bat.) John said that the actual barrel length can be 12", 13", or 14", with most players preferring the longer barrel length.

Avis Vaught told me that most of the women also use a 34" composite bat, 26 or 27 ounce; a few of the women use a 25 ounce bat.

Now, the bats can be end-loaded or balanced. On the end-loaded bats John said that there is a ½ to 1-ounce weight placed in the end of the bat just under the barrel cap. The balanced bats have the weight evenly distributed along the barrel. Some players swear by balanced bat weights; others prefer the end-loaded bats. It's just individual preference, although for the elite players, I'm sure there are good reasons for which bats they choose. For me, it seems like I always hit better with a balanced bat. And I seem to generate more bat speed with a 26 ounce bat than a 28 ounce bat, for instance. But a lot of my friends use a 28 ounce bat.

John said that the average recreation league bats for most players should hold up for approximately 2,500 hits. For the elite, heavy hitters this might be as low as 1,000 hits, he said. John also told me that for most of us, though, a bat should hold up for at least nine of the three-month seasons (three years). The bat I am currently using is now entering its fourth year, so maybe this season will be its last. Fingers crossed on that! But maybe it's time to start looking around for a newer bat. The companies seem to improve them often.

Balls

The balls for all men's leagues are 12-inch balls. The women's leagues use an 11-inch ball. There are a few separate brands, but I don't know much about the differences in compression, hardness, flight distances, etc. I suppose there are some noticeable differences.

I think the men's Rec and Neighborhood leagues use the ASA-sanctioned Trump brand softballs; the RBL and 68+ leagues use ASA-sanctioned Champro balls; CFL currently uses a Trump ball, although at various times they have also used the Baden brand and the Tattoo ball; some other leagues and travel tourneys may vary.

The local ladies leagues use the Trump brand ball, but some of their travel tournaments also use Tattoo, Baden, or the Green Dot softball by Worth.

Officially, compression is a measure of how hard the softball is. The higher the compression, the harder the ball and, generally, the faster and farther it will fly. Compression is measured by how many pounds of force are needed to squeeze two sides of the ball in by a total of one-quarter inch. Commit that to memory, all of you physics majors.

Mostly for me, no matter which ball is being used, I just try to hit it hard or to place it toward a certain area on the field. I think that's the way most players look at it.

There's the old adage, "See the ball. Hit the ball."
Enough said.

Other Equipment

Face masks for pitchers are required in some leagues
and highly recommended in all leagues. Many infielders
use face masks, too, especially at the third and first base
positions. Some other infielders and a few outfielders
also use masks.

Shin guards, knee pads, and ankle protectors are used
by many players, as well as protective cups by the men.
The full, catcher-type shin guards are used primarily by
the pitchers, some of whom also wear chest protectors.
You can barely find a player who doesn't wear some
type of leg brace; knee, ankle, or elbow support; or
something similar.

Metal cleats are not allowed on the shoes.

Special Rules/pitchers/screens

The Rec and Neighborhood leagues generally have
rosters of 12 players and when all players are present,
they must all play, bat, and sit out no more than one
inning. This often results in a manager designating a
rotational player or rover who plays a different position
each inning. This allows the manager to sit a different
player from inning to inning. Some leagues and travel
teams don't follow this pattern, but do often have other
rules governing extra players, extra hitters, substituting,
designated hitters, and so on.

In order to pitch, you must be certified by one of the evaluators. I was evaluated and approved several years ago, although I have only pitched two games. I can't remember precisely how I was evaluated, but I think I had to hit the plate with 15 out of 20 pitches or something like that.

The standard distance from the pitcher's mound to the plate is 50'. You can pitch from behind the mound up to a maximum distance that is marked by a chalk line on the ground.

The arc on pitches must be between 6 and 12 feet; otherwise the pitch is called 'illegal' by the ump and is a ball, even if it hits the plate. A batter can, however, swing at and hit an illegal pitch at his or her discretion, as long as they stay in the batter's box. I have seen batters get some pretty nice hits from pitches that had been called illegal by the umpire.

Screens are often required in certain leagues or at certain tournaments. Screens can pretty much be used in any league, if requested by the pitcher. Most times if a batted ball hits the screen, it is a dead ball and does not count as a strike or ball. In some leagues, or especially in some tournaments, if you hit the screen twice in a row or three times in a row, it is an out. I have even heard of one tournament where the screen is in play and the pitcher must come around and get the ball to make a play; or the ball is also in play if it caroms off the metal support for the screen. But for the most part, hitting the screen results in a no-call, dead ball. Managers will keep you abreast of particular rules for various leagues and tournaments involving the use of screens.

A few leagues, such as the Neighborhood leagues and Rec 1, as well as certain tournaments, will start the batters with a 1-ball, 1-strike count, rather than a 0-0 count. This helps speed up play. You may run into an occasional 'one-pitch' tournament where the batter starts with a 3-2 full count. This puts considerable pressure on both the batter and the pitcher, but definitely speeds up the game. Just about every league and tournament has the rule where if the batter hits a foul ball after a two-strike count, he or she is out. However, I'm told that may occasionally vary with a few tournaments or leagues across the country.

Infield fly

This varies somewhat, as to whether or not it is used, but most leagues employ the infield fly rule. An infield fly is a <u>fair</u> fly ball (not a line drive) that, in the judgment of the umpire, can be caught by an infielder, pitcher, or catcher with ordinary effort and when there are runners on first and second base; or first, second, and third base; and with less than two outs. Base runners can generally tag up and advance at their own risk. Foul pop ups are not supposed to be subject to the infield fly rule, although I noticed some confusion about that in one league a few years ago. A few leagues do not use the infield fly rule at all. Check with your manager.

Sliding

This varies by league, by Division, and by tournament. Generally, the higher level leagues and tournaments do allow sliding, while the lower levels do not. Most leagues that are comprised of Division 1 and 2 players allow sliding into second and third bases.

If you happen to overrun a base while making a turn, in most leagues you can dive or slide back to that base. You cannot, however, slide into home plate in any of the leagues or tournaments.

You'll find out for sure which leagues allow sliding and which don't once you get involved in softball here. As for me, I'm not sliding. Like I told one of my coaches, "if you see me on the ground at second or third base, then just assume that I fell down. I didn't slide."

Home plate, Batter's Box, Bases

On local recreation department fields, the batter's box is a 3' X 7' rectangle marked by white lines on a larger green, artificial turf mat. Some leagues require the batter to stay within the 3' X 7' box when swinging, while others allow the batter to utilize the larger, full mat. This has been the one rule where I have witnessed the most controversial calls here.

A few umps are very strict and will call a batter out if he or she even barely steps out of the box during a swing. Other umps are less strict on that call. It's an umpire's discretion. Personally, I would never call a batter out for this infraction unless he or she either takes steps out of the box toward the pitcher to hit a ball; or steps onto or across the plate to hit a ball. But that's just me.

In our leagues, the pitcher throws to a wooden plate that is a 19" X 34" rectangle. This is what the batters consider the hitting plate. If a pitched ball lands on this plate or hits off of one of the edges, it is a strike.

When a runner rounds third and heads toward home, he or she does not run toward the wooden hitting plate to score. They must run toward a traditional size home plate, which is offset several feet to the runner's right of the wooden plate, in order to score a run. The direction for the runner is generally designated by a white chalk line.

All plays at home plate are force plays. No sliding is allowed. The catcher must field a thrown ball with his or her foot contacting the wooden plate in order to get the runner out.

This is often a difficult call on close plays for the umpire to determine whether the runner has scored or not, since the umps must watch both the wooden plate and the runner's plate in order to make the correct call.

There is a 'commitment line' marked perpendicular to the foul line about 30' from home plate. Once runners cross that line heading to score a run, they cannot return to third base; they must continue home. Also, after crossing the commitment line, the runner cannot be tagged out by a defensive player. The defense must touch the wooden hitter's plate in order to get the runner out.

The bases at third and second are the traditional white color and 15" square. At first base, there are two bases side-by-side. A second base, also 15" square and a darker color, usually orange, is placed in foul territory beside the white base. A runner trying to beat out an infield grounder runs to the orange bag, whereas the fielder attempts the force out by having his or her foot on the white bag. This set-up is intended to minimize collisions and is a safety feature. If a runner is attempting to gain an extra base hit, he or she can touch the inside white base with their foot, as they turn and proceed toward second base. Of course, the first baseman must not interfere with the runner in these instances and allow them plenty of room to run.

Runners

The base paths on our local fields are 65' long. In leagues that do not allow sliding, the runner must veer off or give him or herself up, to avoid collisions at second and third base, but only if a play is being made on the runner. Of course, if it looks like you can get to the bag ahead of the throw, you can go straight toward the base. This creates a few arguments and judgment calls by the umpires. But the rule is well intended and is in place as a safety precaution.

In the leagues where sliding is allowed, you can have rundowns, much like in baseball. But in the no-sliding leagues, you can only return toward a base one time – no rundowns are allowed.

As for substitute runners, there are a variety of rules in place for various leagues:

-In a few leagues runners, who are stationed behind a line off to the side near the backstop, are allowed to run for the batter. I believe that in most of these instances the runner can only advance to first base.

-In most leagues, however, a substitute runner can only be used after the batter has safely reached base.

-In some leagues substitute runners can be used for players who have hit doubles or even triples.

-In other leagues substitute runners can only be used for those who have hit a single. If you hit a double or triple, you must continue to run for yourself.

-In some leagues the same substitute runner can be used once every inning. In other leagues the same substitute runner is limited to twice per game.

-In most leagues, but not all of them, batters who are going to need substitute runners must be designated as such on the lineup cards prior to the game starting.

These substitute runner rules can get confusing, so this is definitely one area you will need to talk to your manager about once you begin to play softball here.

Mercy Rules/Catch-Up Rules

Generally speaking, in most local leagues you can win the game if, after five or more complete innings, you are ahead by 15 or more runs. One league was using 12 runs as a mercy rule for awhile. In some leagues or tournaments in various places, I have heard that you may run into situations where there are no mercy rules.

In most leagues you can only score five runs per inning, until the final inning, which is considered an unlimited scoring inning. Some leagues had a catch-up rule for awhile, where as long as you were behind by more than five runs in any inning, you could continue scoring runs until you caught up.

Some leagues have a rule where, if you are behind by more than five runs in any inning, you can score 'five plus one' or six runs.

Things do vary considerably, and seem to change from time to time; so again, check with your manager or veteran players to find out the situation for your league.

Subs

The use of substitute players varies considerably from league to league. In some leagues you can show up at the fields and sign up to be a last minute sub, if one is needed.

In other leagues if a manager knows ahead of time that he or she will need a sub, they let someone designated by the Board know, and a sub will be contacted and provided for that particular team.

Because of last minute illnesses or in the case of an injury during a game, it is always good to have potential subs on hand to fill in. All care is given to try and provide equal talent for use as subs, but occasionally it becomes whoever is available. In one league I play in, host teams, which are providing umps, scorekeepers, and announcers, also must designate one or two players who are to be available as last minute subs, if needed.

Also, in most of the leagues, new players who have just come out of softball evaluations are given priority on the substitute lists. Of course, also, substitute pitchers are often difficult to come by and are in high demand. I remember one league game where a pitcher got hurt and couldn't continue. The shortstop came in to pitch, and a substitute player was chosen who could, luckily, play shortstop.

It's kind of difficult for newcomers to understand the ins and outs of substitute players, but you will soon figure it out for your particular league and division by talking with other players and managers.

Board of Directors

Most leagues are run by a Board of Directors which is comprised of about nine members. Some leagues have fewer Board members. One I know of has three members and I think there is one with either five or seven Board members.

In one league, I know that the managers comprise most of the Board members. In other leagues Board members are elected by vote of the players. The duration of service varies, but I think most Boards include members who serve two or three year staggered terms.

The Boards help establish rules, rule changes, drafting procedures, schedules, player ratings, and so on.

Sometimes the lead person in a league is called the Commissioner; other times I have heard them referred to as President of their respective league.

Umpires, Scorekeepers, Announcers

I was able to talk with Wayne Lockman about **umpiring** in our local leagues. Wayne serves as the Umpire in Chief for men's Division 3 Recreation Softball.

The recreation and neighborhood leagues, as well as most other leagues playing on Villages fields, utilize volunteers for umpires. Generally, these are also players, but not always. Some of the off-site leagues and special leagues pay umpires.

In all cases, the leagues try to utilize the best and most experienced umpires, whenever possible. Some of the umps are certified at various levels of softball and baseball or have been in the past, but it is not a requirement for our leagues.

Bill Johnson serves as the Umpire in Charge for all of The Villages® softball. He puts on three clinics each year for the umpires and players. These clinics are held during the months between seasons. Bill stresses proper positioning for umpires and explains any recent rule changes that have occurred.

During the practice week prior to the Rec 3 seasons beginning, Wayne will go from field to field and talk with all teams, answer questions, explain new items, etc. He said that there have not been any major rule changes in the last year or so. The Umpire in Chief for each league and division will generally do something similar for their teams.

The official on-the-field clinics are open to players, as well as umpires, and are very instructive, particularly when new or varying rules are being implemented. They also serve as refreshers for umpire positioning on the field during specific situations; emphasizing taking the time to 'make the right call' versus the temptation of making a quick call; and other important items.

I have attended a few of these clinics and they are very informative. Bill and the Chief Umpires are very knowledgeable and really know what they're doing.

The umpires follow the USSSA Senior Softball Rule Book for most things and then follow any special rules that are put in place for individual leagues here locally.

Scorekeepers and **scoreboard operators** are most generally volunteers and are selected from designated host teams which are not playing that particular game. Scorekeepers, announcers, and scoreboard operators sit in towers situated centrally behind the backstops.

Some leagues use a computer system for recording hits and other stats, including a display of where a batter's hits went to on the field (for Rec 3). Some leagues do not keep stats, hits, or anything other than the game scores.

Most of the scoreboards are electronic and are located just outside the centerfield fence. The scoreboards indicate the score by visitors and home teams; the inning; and the number of outs.

Some leagues utilize an **announcer** for the hitter; the on-deck batter; and even for the next batter after that, who is 'in the hole.' Other leagues do not utilize announcers.

Miscellaneous

Temperatures: Andrew Esposito recently told me that the Recreation Department "strongly recommends suspending or cancelling play for these temperatures:

- 35 degrees or below; wind chill not considered, just straight temperature;
- 104 degree heat index or above."

In the seven years I've been here, I've never seen game time temperatures at the lower level. (Of course, since I have my own health issues when temperatures are in the low 60s or below, I generally do not play on those days anyway.) I have been involved in a couple of games, however, when the heat index rose to 104 or 105 degrees and, by vote of the teams playing, we decided to suspend play for the rest of that day.

You will pay for your **shirts and hats** in most leagues. Some sponsored leagues will provide those items (paid for, of course, by the sponsors).

In Neighborhood and Rec leagues the **balls** are furnished, but in many of the other leagues players have to chip in a few bucks each to cover the cost of balls (unless covered by sponsors in some leagues.)

Costs for **travel team uniforms** are usually covered by sponsors, as are entry fees for tournaments. Players in the Half Century League must pay a lifetime registration fee (I think at one time it was $50) and they are then provided with an ID card which must be shown to tournament officials when requested.

There may be a few other odds and end expenses that come up from time to time, but those are some general thoughts on how shirts, hats, balls, and various fees are covered. Prices may change and other circumstances may change, so don't hold me to the above as gospel.

We all also thank those folks who operate the **concession stands** at Buffalo Glen, Saddlebrook, and Everglades. I'm most familiar with Betty Camporeale who has run concessions at Buffalo Glen for the past 11 years. Softball player Larry Rivellese assists Betty with many of her tasks, including repairs, delivering items, etc.

Jenny Ensminger currently handles concessions at Saddlebrook. She took it over from Marla Paras, who had done that for several years. Kim and Alan Martens recently began operating the concession stand at Everglades. All of these folks do an excellent job and this is a valuable service for the players and fans alike.

The employees who perform **field maintenance** are outstanding, too. Currently, those Rec Department employees include Skip Thompson, Tasha White, Ron Miller, Rich Oliva, Vincent DeRobertis, and Steve Stein. Duties include: lining the fields, cleaning the strike mats, putting out practice balls, setting up the scoreboards, checking the sound system; some are also trained in CPR and using the AED machines.

Contractors also do much of the field maintenance, including mowing, dragging the fields, and taking care of the sprinkler systems. At present, those contractor employees are: Austin Welling at Everglades; Kevin Askin at Soaring Eagle; Bobby Shacter at Buffalo Glen; and Deano Morrell at Saddlebrook. Maintenance employees change from time to time, so it is difficult to always keep track of who is handling certain tasks.

Longtime maintenance person, Charlie Monton, was a fixture at the fields until he retired in a ceremony held at Knudson Field on February 26, 2020. Charlie is also featured in a Bio in the Appendix of this book, since he was also a player here from 1997-2009. Because Charlie became almost legendary around the softball scene here and was well known by so many players, I thought I'd give you a short blurb on him. Here are some of the things that Charlie recently told me:

Charlie said he was born in Custer, Michigan in 1933. He told me that there were Native American teepees within sight of their family farm when he was young. If you get the idea that Charlie is full of some interesting stories, you'd be right. That part of Michigan is within the area of the current Huron-Manistee National Forest. His parents later moved about 12 miles west to Ludington, MI, not far from the shore of Lake Michigan, where they farmed and Charlie farmed for the next several decades. Charlie's grandparents were from Belgium and France and they were farmers, too.

Charlie never played sports growing up. "Too busy working on the farm," he said recently. "We had pigs, chickens, and you name it at first. Later, we became dairy farmers with Holstein cows."

"I learned to play softball after my wife and I moved here in 1995," Charlie told me. "I played in various leagues at Knudson and Saddlebrook from 1997 to 2009, when health issues forced me to give up playing."

"I had also started helping out around the Knudson Field around 1998 and I continued doing that on a volunteer basis until 2004, when The Villages® put me on their payroll," Charlie explained. "Since I worked for them, they let me play in the Employee Softball League, also. I really enjoyed that."

"Mostly I would 'line' the field at Knudson, put bases down and just oversee and keep an eye on things," he explained. "I never dragged the fields. Other people did that. I reported any major maintenance needs to my supervisor, which over the years has been John Rohan, Jack Ware, and Danny Jacobs."

After Saddlebrook opened up in 2000, Charlie also helped with maintenance there, as well as at Buffalo Glen after it opened in 2007. He told me that before he retired, he even did some weekend maintenance for tournaments at Soaring Eagle after it opened in 2015.

Pam Henry recently told me that Knudson, the original Villages softball field, was first opened for play in 1984. Charlie did not arrive here until 1995, but he has heard a lot of stories from those who were first here. Many of those oldtimers told him that before Knudson opened for play that they would often practice and hit softballs in an open area down near the current archery range. He said they also told him that at one time there was a tree in center field at Knudson and many of the batters would aim for it before it was finally removed.

Charlie said that since the Knudson fence is only a distance of 228 feet, that especially after the newer "hot" bats began to become available, as well as premier softballs, many hitters would hit home runs out into the road or even across it.

"Thank goodness Saddlebrook opened in 2000 with the 300-foot fence," Charlie said. "The better players and power hitters all started playing over there. Then they also started using non-composite bats and a lesser ball for the Knudson games. Even then, a few players could still hit home runs," Charlie recalled.

"The Knudson field was a little ragged back in the early days," Charlie said. "It's in great shape now compared to back then."

"The softball fields became my second home and the players were like family to me," Charlie said. "I hated to retire, but I guess age (87) just finally caught up with me. It's going to be hard for me to stay away."

Charlie Monton certainly became a legend around the softball fields. I suspect that even now, if you notice a small, older gentleman, sitting in the stands watching a game at the Knudson Field, you might very well discover that his name is Charlie Monton. Thank you for your contributions over the years, my friend.

III. PRIMARY LEAGUES AND DIVISIONS

When I talk about 'primary' leagues, I'm basically referring to the official leagues sponsored by the Recreation Department – those are the Recreation (Rec) Leagues and the Neighborhood Leagues.

In this chapter I will first discuss the men's recreation and neighborhood leagues. And you will see that the neighborhood 4 and 5 leagues also include the women, so I have included some information from Jane Girotti about that.

This chapter also includes a section about the women's leagues. There is some information from Avis Vaught about the Ladies Divisions 1, 2, and 3 Recreation Leagues, as well as some background and history of the overall ladies programs from Pam Henry, Judy Wanko, Jan Washburn, and Darlene Hedrick.

I hope this chapter gives all newcomers, who may be interested in playing softball here, an idea of the basic softball opportunities that are available to them.

MEN'S

I'd like to thank Vernon Brooks, Ron Lottes, Dave Mamuscia, Bob Hrabak, Joe Sanchez, Wally Dias, Dick Kanyan, Wayne Meyer, Dave Bigelow, Doug White, Jack Nagle, Jack Kleffman, and Bill DiCarlo for their input about the men's leagues in this chapter. I hope I didn't miss mentioning anyone in this list; but if I did, they are likely mentioned elsewhere in the book. And again, Jane Girotti has provided information concerning the ladies participation in the neighborhood Co-Ed leagues, N4 and N5.

For the men there are six Rec leagues and five divisions: Rec 1, Rec 2, Rec 3, Rec 4, Rec 5, and the Knudson (K) Rec 5 league; and there are four Neighborhood (N) leagues: N 1/2, N3, N4, and N5. As previously noted, N4 and N5 are actually Co-Ed leagues.

All of those various leagues and divisions listed above are run by separate Boards elected by the players. There are generally 9 members for each Board. As mentioned in the previous chapter, the Boards help establish rules, rule changes, drafting procedures, schedules, player ratings, and so on.

RECREATION LEAGUES

If you've ever played organized softball anywhere else around the country, you will generally find things here are very similar in terms of the game itself. You will likely see, however, that the facilities and the overall organization are possibly even better than what you have been used to. That goes for the players, too. There are some really good players here.

Many of the specific differences that are found here overall, as well as between leagues and divisions, have been mentioned in the previous chapter. So, I won't duplicate all of that here. Those were the discussions about bats, runners, equipment, balls, evaluations, drafts, screens, masks, sliding, and so forth. But there are a few additional things mentioned in this chapter that I hope you will find useful to know.

Also, I have included some comments and information from players and managers about their respective leagues that you will find interesting.

And as I've said before and will probably do so again, since nothing much is set in stone in terms of some of these rules, you'll just have to find out about them once you start playing. I do guarantee you two things: 1) it's still mostly just basic softball; and 2) certain things will change every year, if not every season.

As of the winter 2020 season, Rec 1 and Rec 2 played twice a week – on Wednesday and Friday mornings; Rec 3 and Rec 4 played twice a week – on Monday and Thursday mornings; Rec 5 played twice a week – on Tuesday and Friday mornings; and Rec K5 played three times a week – on Monday, Wednesday, and Thursday mornings. During the summer seasons Rec K5 usually plays only on Monday and Thursday.

From season to season the Rec 1-5 leagues generally alternate between the Saddlebrook and Buffalo Glen fields, which were discussed in the previous chapter. The Knudson Rec league, of course, plays its games at the Knudson field, which was also previously discussed. Occasionally, the Rec field rotations can change, but in general, this is how it has run for the seven years or so that I have played here. Any location changes that are made are publicized ahead of time and league officials and managers keep the players well informed.

(**A Side Note**: Some of the ladies leagues, including Tri-County, play at Soaring Eagle. However, as noted in the next chapter, the Tri-County league only plays one season a year, from December through about mid-March. Ladies clinics and open play have also been scheduled at Soaring Eagle. The men's 68+ league plays at Soaring Eagle. More on this later.)

With the opening of the Everglades softball complex in the new section of The Villages® community a few months ago, there may be some changes made to several league schedules in the future; but this has not been determined at this time. Everglades is a very nice complex with four beautiful fields. It is located south of Rt. 44 down toward the Fenney area. The Central Florida League (CFL) moved its games from Saddlebrook to the Everglades fields beginning with the winter 2020 season.

Here is the miscellaneous information that I promised earlier about the men's recreation leagues:

Rec 1 – Dave Mamuscia said that playing in this league "has been great for him!" He told me that "I was a pretty ordinary player when younger (and still am). I never imagined being able to play this much softball through my mid-70s with players who perform at such a high level. It's been a dream come true," he said.

Dave continued, "Perhaps our greatest strength, and from talking with players in other leagues I think this is true throughout, is the process for selecting teams to ensure competitive balance. Also, when the teams are re-drafted three times each year, you get to meet and play with a wide variety of other players. The system of Divisions allows players to compete with others of similar abilities and skills, so that everyone can enjoy the game and not feel out of place," he said.

Dave noted that several players, who began in Rec 1 or Rec 2 when they were younger, have continued to play into their mid to late 80s at Knudson. He views this as one of the best aspects of softball here: that you can pretty much continue playing as long as you desire and are able. There's a league for everyone.

Dave also wanted me to mention that this league now employs the 1-1 pitch rule – all batters start with a one ball, one strike count on them. This generally speeds up play.

Rec 2 – Dick Kanyan told me that he has only played in Recreation 2 for a few seasons. "But I can tell you that this is a well oiled machine," he said. "I've been extremely impressed with the Board in handling their duties, the training they provide for score keeping, the managers, and the quality of play in this league."

Rec 3 – Ron Lottes told me that Rec 3 was the first league to develop computer scoring and tracking for statistics. He said that John Fink took the lead on this for technical development; Wally Dias handled certain administrative matters, including getting WiFi installed at the fields; and now Chuck Bowler oversees the various tasks. Dias told me that Ron Lottes purchased and donated the first four computers used for R3 scoring and tracking.

Doug White is also heavily involved in this computer tracking system. He recently told me, "I enjoy volunteering as a computer scorekeeper for the R3 league. We score the details of each game and record the plays; hit position; hit type; and then submit the score sheets to the local newspaper. Managers can access every player's hit location, 'spray' diagram, and other batting stats to get an idea of what defensive strategy might work against each batter," White said.

Rec 4 – Bob Hrabak told me that Rec 4 went to a computerized statistics system beginning in 2019.

I recently talked with Dave Bigelow, who is the R4 President. He has been involved with R4 since 2006.

Dave told me that the computerized system mentioned above is working well, but that they are "continuing to refine a few things." He said that "the previous system was a little cumbersome. This new system," Bigelow continued, "keeps track of things as they happen; it more or less gives us instant stats. We're still trying to get a few more trained volunteers to help with it, but overall we are very pleased."

Dave said the R4 league is competitive, but fun. "We have great camaraderie among the players. We've been really glad to get back to playing softball recently after the corona virus had things shut down for several weeks," he said.

Rec 5 – Wayne Meyer has served on the Board and as Commissioner for this league. He said, "I've often been called the Chief Cook and Bottle Washer! You'll meet a broad spectrum of guys in this league from long-time players to more recent players," Wayne told me. "Many of us are not as good as we used to be, but we keep some stats and have great fun. We're legends in our own minds," he laughed.

Substitute runners are allowed in Rec 5 once the batter reaches any base safely. See further info on that rule in the Rec K5 write-up below and in the N5 section.

Wayne said that, depending upon the season, they usually have between 8 and 18 teams in the league. "We even have a 90 year old pitcher, Dale Appleby, in our league," said Meyer. Hats off to Dale!

Rec K5 – Runners are allowed to run for the batter in this Knudson league and also in N5 – from behind and off to the side of the batter's box. The runner can only advance to first base, no matter how far the batter hits the ball. Here's the way the rule reads for the Knudson R5 league:

COURTESY RUNNERS (from home plate):

A) A courtesy runner from home plate must remain on the courtesy runner's plate until the batter swings at a pitched ball. The batter shall be called out if the runner violates this rule.
B) A courtesy runner starting from home plate will be limited to one base only (1st base). If the courtesy runner inadvertently draws a throw from running towards another base, the courtesy runner and any preceding runners will be returned to the last occupied base.

This special courtesy runner rule is also used in the N5 league, but is a little more complicated there.

Bats in the K5 league are all one and two-piece 1.20 BPF; no composite 1.21 BPF bats are allowed. The ball is less lively, too. Despite these things, a few home runs are still hit at Knudson each season over the 228-foot fence.

One player in this league is in his 90s and several are in their 80s. Joe Sanchez estimates the average age is about 76 or 77. Sanchez says, "This league is the last stop for many players. Eventually, injuries and age catch up with all of us. In some ways this is a more relaxed league, but you would be surprised at how competitive some of these players still are," he told me.

NEIGHBORHOOD LEAGUES

The Neighborhood leagues all play on Saturday mornings at the Saddlebrook and Buffalo Glen locations. Two things that you will notice right off the bat, so to speak, are:

1) The hitters start with a one-ball, one-strike count on them. This is intended to speed up play, but takes a little getting used to, especially if you are one of those batters who likes to 'take' the first pitch. Do that in this league and you may find yourself way behind in the count and having to 'protect the plate' on the next pitch. Then if it's close, you'll have to swing at it or risk striking out. Because of that, many batters will swing at the first pitch, if it is anywhere close to the plate.

2) The bats are furnished in all divisions except the Neighborhood 1/2 league. And these furnished bats are

Easton, single-wall aluminum, 1.20 BPF. There is no 'pop' to them, like the composite bats that are used in most of the other leagues. But it does somewhat even out the velocity of the balls coming back at the pitcher and to the infielders. Plus, there aren't nearly as many long balls hit over the heads of the outfielders. It makes for a safer game. And after all, these leagues are intended to be more laid back games between players who are friends and neighbors. That doesn't mean that players aren't competitive. They still try to play well and win, but it is certainly done in a spirit of camaraderie and good sportsmanship.

As mentioned previously, I understand that the Division 1/2 neighborhood league players are now allowed to use their own bats; and those can be two-piece, similar to the RBL, as long as the bat is ASA rated and the compression ratio is 1.20 BPF.

Some of the ladies play on the men's teams in the Neighborhood 4 and 5 Divisions. They play quite well and very competitively. Many of these ladies have played softball for years and are very skilled. When men are batting in these Co-Ed Neighborhood Leagues, they use the 12" ball. When the ladies bat, they use the 11" softball.

As the name implies, most of the teams in these leagues come from within the same neighborhoods. However, some neighborhoods don't have enough players for a full roster. In many of those cases, two neighborhoods will combine to form a team.

Sometimes, there may only be one or two players from a certain neighborhood who want to play in this league. Those players are generally assigned to a team that may be just a player or two short of having a full roster. That happened to me. I live in Dunedin and we didn't have but a couple of Division 3 softball players living here when I began playing Neighborhood; so I was assigned to the St. Charles team, where I played for several seasons. It worked out well and I still have many friends from that team. I know of a couple more Dunedin residents who have played N3 for Collier and Lake Deaton.

Rest assured, if you want to play Neighborhood ball, the league officials will find you a team.

I've been told that the Neighborhood League idea began back in the late 1990s when a group of guys from the Palo Alto Club, led by Jack Augustine, began to gather and play at the Knudson Field. Before long they started playing against guys from Hacienda.

When the Saddlebrook fields opened in 2000, play also included teams from Santiago, Mira Mesa, and Santo Domingo. Some of those early organizers, besides Augustine, included George Rodriguez, Don Bowman, Joe Sanchez, and Dick Johnson, among others.

Pretty soon, in addition to these teams, there were even 30 or 40 other players who wanted to sub whenever possible. By the fall of 2000 there were as many as eight teams wanting to play on Saturday mornings, and this became the basis of the Neighborhood League.

Around 2001, the Recreation Department got involved and things grew. It wasn't long before there was something like 24 teams, organized play, a governing Board, and rules.

Other key individuals in the early days were Terry Cole, Bob Pasqua, and Nelson Samler.

The early leaders of the league credit John Rohan, who leads the Recreation Department, for coming up with the idea to use a consistent, single-wall bat among all the teams. The bats are now supplied by the Recreation Department and the teams share a group of bats each game.

A few players who didn't like to use these 'dead' bats dropped out. But as many of the early league leaders noted, this was just a friendly once a week league among neighbors. They only wanted to get together and have an enjoyable time playing softball like they did when they were kids, regardless of what type of bat was being used. It has worked out well.

Years ago, Sanchez noted, the league was popular with those who didn't participate in the Recreation Leagues or on the Travel Teams. Also, it was good for those people who still worked at jobs and could not play softball during the week. And there was a place for players of all skill levels. This concept is still in place today, although there are many more players and teams involved, including those who also play in numerous other leagues during the week.

With the more laid back atmosphere and with batted balls not coming at fielders nearly as fast as in other leagues, it gives people a chance to get back in a more gradual way to playing softball, especially if they haven't played in many years.

I'd like to thank Jack Nagle who provided me with much of the information on the last two pages.

Here is the miscellaneous information that I promised earlier about the men's neighborhood leagues. And as noted earlier, some of the ladies play in the N4 and N5 leagues, making these Co-Ed leagues:

N1/2 – I talked with Bill DiCarlo about this league. I've known Bill since 2015 after he first moved here. We played together in the RBL. He's a very good player and his Bio is included in the Appendix.

Bill said that there are fewer participants in this league than the other Neighborhood Leagues. The league is for the higher skill levels, which influences the number of players available.

The teams are composed regionally, rather than by individual village, and the league normally has from four to seven teams competing. Recent teams have included: Winifred, 466 North, Brownwood, Buena Vista East, Buttonwood, 466 South, 44 South; or depending upon the season, the number of players available, and where the individual players live, there have been combinations of some of these teams.

The Saturday morning league permits those that still work during the week a place to participate and meet others prior to retiring full-time.

Unlike other Neighborhood leagues, rather than using Villages-supplied bats, ASA 1.20 rated bats are used. When you first start playing, your teammates will gladly share their bats with you. There is no need to purchase an ASA bat solely for this league, until you are sure you are going to continue playing in N1/2.

Bill noted that "although games are often very competitive, no player statistics are maintained; so, you will find this league to be more lighthearted than the twice a week Recreation league competitions. Also, by combining Recreation League Division 1 and 2 players on teams, it helps expand your circle of friends and contacts outside of the Rec leagues," he said.

N3 – Vernon Brooks, who coached and played on the Neighborhood Division 3 Sanibel team for a number of years, recently told me that he considers the Neighborhood Leagues a "good place to start for those who have never played much softball or who have not played for many years."

As noted earlier, since the Neighborhood leagues use the single-wall aluminum bats, the rebound speed of the softballs is considerably slower than in the leagues which use the composite bats. If a new player, who hasn't played softball for many years, chooses to play in these leagues, he may find it easier to get back in the 'swing of things', so to speak, before transitioning to the leagues that use the "hotter" composite bats.

N4 – Jack Kleffman has played in several leagues and several Divisions. He told me that in some seasons there are as many as 24+ teams in the N4 league. He considers it a very fun league. Jack has played Neighborhood ball for Springdale for 12 years. He said that there are some very good hitters and fielders in this league; and that the main difference between N4 and the next higher league is that most players don't run as fast as they once did. Jack has also been involved with player evaluations for 15 years.

N5 – In a recent telephone conversation, Joe Sanchez told me that he was one of the original four men who started the Neighborhood Leagues idea at Knudson in the late 1990s, along with Don Bowman, Dick Johnson, and Jack Augustine. They formed a team named Orange Blossom. This team continues to play in Neighborhood 5 to this day and is still comprised of many of the best players from the original Knudson group. The N5 league might have anywhere from 8-12 teams in any particular season and the Orange Blossom squad has won the league title more often than not.

Joe told me that "the commitment and time donated by the various softball volunteers: managers, board members, umpires, scorekeepers, announcers, and others are truly amazing. Together they make things operate very smoothly."

As noted in the earlier section about the Knudson Rec 5 league, courtesy runners for the batter are also allowed in N5. The N5 rule is similar to the Rec K5 league rule, but is a little more involved, Sanchez told me.

It's not the intent of this book to delve too deeply into the rules of the various leagues (you will find that they do differ considerably on many items.) When you decide to play in these various leagues, you can get a quick indoctrination from managers and veteran players into specific rules. Rest assured, however, as I have mentioned previously, it is still just softball.

Jane Girotti, whose Bio is included in the Appendix, has provided the following information about the Co- Ed participation in N4 and N5:

Neighborhood Co-Ed Softball by Jane Girotti

"From the beginning neighborhood teams were designed for co-ed participation. For the gals the struggle to be embraced and accepted by all participants has become easier over the last few years.

As there are more men's divisions than ladies divisions, the ladies participation has pretty much been only in Neighborhood 4 and 5. All three of the ladies league divisions qualify to play in Neighborhood 4 or 5. Ladies 1 must play in N4 and Ladies 2 can play either in N4 or N5; Ladies 3 must play in N5.

Originally, N4 and N5 played as one combined division. A few years back these two divisions were split into two individual neighborhood leagues. This was necessary because the combined league was growing so big that it was starting to become more difficult to manage. Plus, the ability disparity between N4 and N5 was becoming increasingly problematic.

Over these last few years the gals have proven they can be very competitive in Neighborhood 4 and 5 leagues. Truthfully, there are a handful of gals that I feel could play at ANY level.

I manage the Duval team in N5 and we certainly hold our own. This summer (2020) my team consists of 7 women and 5 men. We still have teams that consist of all men and I feel that we will become more co-ed as the years go by.

Personally I am happy there is still softball out there to play for someone my age. We are very fortunate to be able to accommodate so many players at so many levels."

WOMEN'S

I'd like to thank Avis Vaught, Pam Henry, Judy Wanko, Jan Washburn, and Darlene Hedrick for contributing to this section.

During the winter 2020 season the Ladies Rec 1, 2, and 3 all played on Tuesdays and Fridays at Buffalo Glen, with some clinics and additional league play on Fridays at Soaring Eagle. Sometimes things change, but you will receive adequate advance notice each season.

As previously covered, many of the women play in the Neighborhood 4 and Neighborhood 5 leagues with the men on Saturday mornings. When batting in these leagues, the ladies hit the 11-inch ball; while the men still hit the 12-inch ball.

Ladies Recreation Softball Leagues

These three leagues play two days a week and have three divisions or skill levels. This ensures that any resident may participate safely in one of the Ladies Divisions.

The program started in the late 1990's with one division and by 2017, with the increased participation of residents, it expanded to three divisions.

Each Division:

1) Has a board that may modify the rules of the game to accommodate that particular level of senior player;

2) Provides all female residents opportunities to play based on an evaluation of her skills and knowledge of play;

3) Has volunteer players who serve on the boards to set the season schedule, draft teams, hold meetings, create social opportunities, etc.

There are also residents who volunteer as scorekeepers, umpires, team managers, evaluators, and to help with clinics. The overall program works with each of the divisions to ensure smooth transitions from one division to another for all players.

The program is not just for playing softball, but for support on and off the diamond; several players told me that it is like having sisters and family to join in various other activities. The Villages Recreation Staff provides guidelines and assistance for all League Division Boards, when needed. Some residents who have come here to play say that "this is Softball Heaven."

Ladies Division 1 - This division is mostly comprised of residents who are in the younger age groups, as well as those with a high level of skill. The players in this division usually have been involved with softball since childhood. This includes those with high school and college playing experience; those who continued to play post-college on tournament teams, in military leagues and employee leagues; and women who have been teachers and coaches at various levels. Many players in this division serve as instructors, providing support, and teaching players in the other divisions.

Ladies Division 2 - This division includes many residents with the same experience as in D1; however, aging may have affected their speed, power, or agility. Also, younger new residents who have not played a lot during their lives, but have had some exposure to organized play are also typical players in D2. Playing rules may be modified so that all players in this league have the opportunity to safely enjoy participating. Clinics are held regularly to assist with skills development of new players and for other players that are interested in advancing their softball abilities.

Ladies Division 3 - This division includes many residents with similar backgrounds as D1 and D2, but perhaps aging or injuries have had an impact on their physical abilities; quite a few of these ladies have had shoulder and knee surgeries or other health issues, but still desire to play softball. D3 also provides opportunities for those new to the game to learn the rules and work on their softball skills. These ladies may not have had the opportunity for high school and collegiate softball in their younger years. This division also modifies the rules, giving all players the opportunity to participate with others who have had to make playing adjustments.

There are scheduled weekly 'open' play times for the women, as well as ladies clinics, and general open play times for all residents who want to work on enhancing their softball skills.

*   *   *   *   *   *

Here is some interesting information on the overall women's program that was furnished to me by Pam Henry of the Recreation Department:

"In the beginning (when I came on board in 1996) Friday morning organized play (for women) at Knudson was in place; I just took over the management. We had anywhere from 15-30 ladies showing up to play. Depending on the number, we would just play hit & catch or divide into teams for a pickup game. Around 1997-98 the ladies who wanted more league play starting playing in a league with Spruce Creek, Plantation, Clerbrook, and one other retirement community - the name escapes me at this time. We continued with the Friday morning organized play and program, starting to group, as new ladies softball players moved into The Villages.

When Saddlebrook came on-line in 2000 we started play there and the ladies led by Aileen Milton, Aileen Laing, and maybe Shirley Jones, requested they be allowed to play with the men since there were not enough ladies to form a league of their own. The ladies were allowed to play with the men in the neighborhood league and still do in lower divisions today.

With the growth of The Villages, more & more ladies softball players now reside here, allowing for a viable, growing ladies softball program.

The Ladies Softball program is a true testament to The Villages® Lifestyle. To see how it has grown from simple organized pick-up ball on Fridays at Knudson to a full-fledged league today is just amazing. To grow from a handful of ladies, who just wanted to play a sport they weren't able to in their past, to the well-established program it is today is an inspiration to us all. It was always, and will always be, a team effort between the Recreation & Parks Department and passionate Villagers."

Most of Pam's remarks above were from the 20th Anniversary Celebration for ladies softball, which was held on March 28, 2019 at the Saddlebrook Fields. Judy Wanko, who served as Chairperson for that event, provided me with a copy of the program for that celebration. The program also included remarks from John Rohan, Scott Grimes, and Danny Jacobs of the Recreation Department, as well as from Nick Feely of The Daily Sun newspaper. This special thank you was included in the official program:

The Celebration is a collaborative effort of many past and current players. A special thank you to Shirley Jones, Denise Emch, Jan Washburn, and all the other ladies who provided contact information, pictures, articles, and stories to make this a special day for all!

*   *   *   *   *   *

Jan Washburn submitted the following history of women's softball in The Villages® Community. It was included in the commemorative program on March 28, 2019:

The Villages Ladies Softball History - In 1996, Pam Henry started her tenure with The Villages® Recreation Department. She took over management of the existing women's softball 'Friday morning organized play,' which was started by resident Betty Josephson at Paradise Rec. Center's Knudson Field. Anywhere from 15 to 30 ladies would show up. Depending on the number, they would play, hit, and catch, or if there were enough players, teams would be formed. The method was for everyone to line up and count off, 1, 2, 1, 2 and so on with all the 1's on one team, all the 2's on the other team. And so it began . . .

The Villages 'Red' Team was formed to play in a league with outside communities in 1996. Several years later, more Villages teams and neighboring communities joined the league, known as the Lake County Ladies Traveling Senior Softball League; the name was changed in 2003 to Tri-County Golden Ladies Softball League, which continued to add teams from The

Villages® community, as well as more outside retirement locations.

As the league grew, division play was added. Today, the Tri-County League consists of three divisions and a total of five teams representing The Villages® community. Ladies continued to look for opportunities to play ball . . . . The Recreation League was formed in 2000 with four teams playing one day a week at Knudson Field. Word spread around the country about the lifestyle and opportunities to play softball here and the ladies recreation league grew by leaps and bounds. Games moved from Knudson Field to include Saddlebrook, Buffalo Glen, and now the Soaring Eagle softball complex.

There are currently 12 teams in three divisions, with a total of 175 active players with games being played two days a week. The Neighborhood Co-Ed League provided another opportunity. Over the years, ladies played with their own neighborhood team or helped out other neighborhood teams. Women players are still involved in this league today. Because 'snowbirds' migrated north during the summer, there weren't enough women to play. In 2003, a few ladies played in the Men's Rec. League Division III. In 2006, eight ladies entered a draft in Division V and were welcomed by the men for their softball skills.

In 2003, our first women's team participated in the National Senior Games at Hampton Roads, Virginia. The team didn't do well, partly because it was their first time playing under lights. But this competition and experience was a door that opened the way to many future local, state and national tournaments for our teams.

A new era of women's softball had evolved. In 2009, yearning for more competitive play, the Xtreme Diamonds League was formed. There were three top-level teams, two from The Villages® community and a team from Del Webb. Ladies softball teams have now represented us in tournaments and games all over the country, spreading the word that this is a great place to retire and play ball ... and it all started with the Recreation Department's direction and support and the desire of a few residents to play softball.

Twenty-three years later, thank you Pam Henry and other Recreation Department employees for assistance with the women's softball program. To those of you on the 1999-2000 honoree list, as well as all the women who have played over the past 20 years and those who are still playing, thank you for your participation and contributions. The Villages® ladies softball program and opportunities to play are alive and well!! It proves the point that past, present and future '*Girls Just Want to Have Fun!*'

From Knudson Field in 1999 to Saddlebrook, to Buffalo Glen, to Soaring Eagle and to fields all across the USA, The Villages® softball ladies play their hearts out representing their hometown. Playing softball here is more than just game, it's an opportunity to develop friendships both on and off the field.

AUTHOR'S NOTE - Darlene Hedrick provided me with the following re-cap of her softball career. She graciously agreed to have it printed in this book. I think readers will find it very interesting. Thank you, Darlene.

My Softball Life
By Darlene Huntsinger Hedrick

I didn't start playing softball until 1971; I was 28 and living in Hawaii at Barbers Point Naval Air Station. Some of the ladies I bowled with started a softball league with military wives and military women. I was asked to play even after I told them I had never played softball before. We were able to create 4 teams. The team I was on was called the "Over The Hill Gang" and we came in last place that season. The first season I played I had pulled muscles and had many bruises. I started out with a used bat and glove that belonged to the rec. department. The next season my team came in first place. I played 2 yrs in Hawaii.

We moved to Norfolk VA in 1973; my husband was stationed on the USS Mount Whitney. As soon as I could, I went out to the softball fields, trying to find a team to play with. I found one and played there for 3 years. They needed a pitcher for the team; luckily I bowled in 3 leagues and softball pitching is about the same as bowling in many ways. We lost some, won some, and some got rained out.

Our next move was in 1976 to the Washington DC Navy Annex. We lived in Woodbridge VA and I found a league there. I was able to play with both of my daughters after they turned 18. For the 30 years that I lived there, I played in many leagues in the Washington DC Area, sometimes up to nine games a week and two practices. I still played softball with one of my daughters until I moved to The Villages in 2005.

When I was 47 in 1990 while living in VA, I thought I would stop playing softball when I turned 50; but that didn't happen. I found an over-40 league called "The Golden Girls." They also had two tournament teams that traveled both in-state and to many other states. At that time there was only a 50+ age bracket for women's teams. The teams were allowed five players that could be 47 years old. Playing with The Golden Girls, we won many tournaments in Canada, PA, CA, TX, UT, WV, NY, NC, AK, TN, WA, VA, AZ, FL, MD, MI, NV, FL, SC and OH (I might have forgotten some of the states.) I played with The Golden Girls of VA until 2008. I'm still a member of that league. This year the Golden Girls will celebrate their 30th anniversary.

Since moving to The Villages in 2005, I have played in Divisions 1, 2, and 3 of the women's softball league. I have also played Tri-County, Neighborhood, and some of the summer months I was able to play with the Men's D5 teams.

In 2008 I was fortunate to be able to join a tournament team here in The Villages® community called the "Vixens." We started going to many of the same tournaments that I went to with my other team, plus a few more new ones. I played with them for three years.

We won every tournament that we entered in those three years.

In 2012 I was fortunate again to be able to join a great team called the "Golden Gals," a tournament team from The Villages® community. We have been winning most of our tournaments. I started playing with them as a 65+, 70+ and now I'm on the 75+ team.

We are so fortunate to live in The Villages to be able to play all year long. I plan on playing softball until I just can't do it anymore.   - Darlene Hedrick.

IV. OTHER LEAGUES AND TEAMS

This chapter deals with the divisions and leagues that play locally, in addition to the Recreation and Neighborhood leagues. This chapter will also briefly discuss the travel/tournament teams, the local annual Veterans tournaments, and the Senior Games.

As with previous chapters, this is but an overview. The intent is to give newcomers and others who are interested in the local softball scene a glimpse of what is available, if you want to play softball here.

I've interviewed several people to try and present you with accurate information. I've done my best with that, but this has been somewhat difficult. Memories fade, and with certain things I've had two or three people give me different perspectives on the same item. I've tried to sort that out the best that I can. Of course, I have played in three of the leagues mentioned below, so that has helped to keep those things straight.

But the bottom line is that this chapter will give you an idea of what is available to you out there. As you get involved with these various teams and softball leagues, you will find out specific details that are in effect at that time. Remember what I've said - it's still just softball.

It is all quite amazing, however: the fields, the volunteers, the overall organization, and of course, the players and managers. I don't think you can go wrong if you decide to pursue playing in any of these leagues or on the tournament/travel teams mentioned below.

68+ League

Matt Spanier recently told me that this league began around 10 years ago and, as the name suggests, it is for players 68 years old or more. Occasionally a 67 year old is allowed to play if he will be turning 68 later that season or before the next season begins. That actually happened to me.

Terry Cole and a couple of other players started the league after talking around and determining the interest level for this age group. Later on, Matt, Larry Liotta, and then Bill Taylor got involved.

In the beginning they played at Saddlebrook in the afternoons. Initially, there were four teams and the players had to be rated as Division 3, 4, or 5 skill level. Fast forward to today and there are usually 10 teams during the winter months and six teams in the summers. Currently, they play one day a week on Wednesday mornings at Soaring Eagle. At this time the league only accepts Division 3 and 4 players, with a few from Division 5 who have been grandfathered-in from the early years.

Most rules for this league are similar to other leagues: they use the standard 12-inch ball; senior softball (composite) bats; umps and tower personnel are volunteers from the teams; no sliding; but as with almost every league here, you will find slight differences. You will find out those things from your manager once you begin play – things like the mercy rule, substitution and courtesy runner rules, catch up rules, etc.

It is mandatory for pitchers to either wear a mask or to pitch from behind a screen. Balls batted into the screen are automatically dead balls and do not count as a strike or ball against the batter. Most pitchers in this league prefer to wear the masks, rather than use the screen.

Spanier considers the 68+ league to be competitive, but fun. "We don't keep stats," he recently told me, "and we may be a little more laid back than most other leagues. But we have fun and all of the guys seem to enjoy playing in the league."

Matt ran the league almost single-handedly for several years, but now a 3-man board helps with things. The current Board includes Matt Spanier, Lindell Grigg, and John Cilento.

I have enjoyed playing in this league for the past 3+ years. Actually, Al Deibler got me involved playing in this league a few years ago. These fields are only a couple of miles from where I live, so it is the most convenient location for me to play at.

Central Florida League (CFL)

I recently talked with Jack Nesci, who has been involved with the Central Florida League (CFL) since its beginning in 2007. Many of the first players had previously been involved with the Mid-Florida League, which has since folded.

The CFL played games at Saddlebrook and initially consisted of players from Divisions 1, 2, and 3. Some of the first CFL organizers and players, according to Nesci, were Ed Moriarity, Bob Winder, Bob Nutoni, Bill

Turechek, John Wyks, Ted Ramirez, Carlos Lopez, Jim Sherman, and Scott Ashton, to name just a few. Today's CFL consists of players from Divisions 2 and 3, as well as a few who are 'grandfathered-in' from Division 1. Since the winter 2020 season, the CFL has played its games at the new Everglades complex south of Rt. 44.

The CFL plays once a week, currently on Tuesday mornings, and has an oversight board consisting of nine members. Most pitchers wear masks, although it is permissible to use screens; you can slide in this league; and they maintain a substantial substitute list. Their long-time umpire in charge is Rick Craze. CFL uses the infield fly rule and a 15-run mercy rule. As with most local leagues, specific rules change from time to time and managers will go over any changes with their teams prior to the start of the season.

I played in this league for several seasons and I thoroughly enjoyed it. As I recall, I have played for Synergy Wealth, IHOP Restaurant, Softball's R Game, Arden Jewelers, and Palm Ridge Dental – good players and quality managers throughout.

Teams are sponsored, in terms of hats and jerseys, by various area businesses.

Classics League (i.e., Classic 70's)

Tom McGann played in this league for several years and he recently filled me in on some of its specifics, as well as providing me with general information on various other softball leagues and travel teams.

I also got information from Frenchie Le Tan, who was Commissioner of this League for several years, as well serving as the long-time coach of the Munn's team. Frenchie goes back in this league to its first days in the early 2000s when players could be 68 and older before it was changed to 70 years and older.

During the winter season of 2020 the Classics League played games on Tuesday afternoons at Saddlebrook. They play one day per week.

As the name 'Classic 70s' suggests, you have to be age 70 or older to play in this league, although you can be 69 if you will be turning 70 in that calendar year. Most of the players in this league are levels Division 1 and 2, with some Division 3. Managers are more or less able to 'recruit' players for their teams; and there always seems to be parity with good players on all teams.

This league requires pitchers to use screens and they use the composite senior softball bats.

Also, currently one team in this league is from Del Webb and at one point there were a few players from Ocala and other locations. But now, all are from The Villages® community, except the Del Webb team. Paid umpires are used in this league and there is usually only one umpire per game. Rosters generally carry 16 players per team. There are a few different rules regarding substitute players, pinch runners, pitch hitters, etc. that can be explained by the managers and long-time players, if you begin playing in this league.

Restricted Bat League (RBL)

Bill Taylor recently told me that this league began around 2006 or 2007. For a year or two before that, several of the players would meet to practice or play pick-up games. He said that Jerry Krebs was the primary organizer. Jerry had been a pitcher in Division 2 and was increasingly concerned with the velocity of batted balls coming back at pitchers in the Recreation Leagues.

So, rather than use the 'super-charged' composite senior softball bats, this league decided to use only single-wall aluminum or steel bats. The intent was to play games with lower velocity bat rebound speeds, as mentioned in a previous chapter. One or two players, I'm told, even used wooden bats for a season or two. Two-piece bats are allowed, as long as the barrel is single-wall aluminum or steel.

One popular bat for years has been the DeMarini 1.20 BPF bat with a composite handle and a single-wall steel barrel. I use one of those bats myself in RBL. It's a good bat, but balls definitely do not fly off them like they do with the composite 1.21BPF bats. The league maintains a list of approved bats for use in RBL.

Bill told me that Mike Hayes, Fred Olivero, and Jack Curley led the league in various early years. Later, Bill's wife, Jeri, began helping run the scoreboards; and eventually Bill and Jeri took over running the league for six or seven years. For the past two or three years Jack Nagle has been the RBL commissioner. His assistants are currently Wayne Grunewald, handling the sub list and procedures; Mike Bernier overseeing the bat approvals; Arnie Bott in charge of uniforms; and Nick Sticco administering the RBL website. These folks, as well as the team managers, comprise the board for RBL.

In the early years there were generally five or six teams in the league. Later, it grew to as many as 10 teams. In the most recent season there were eight teams in the RBL. The league plays its games on Tuesday afternoons at Buffalo Glen during the fall and winter seasons. There is currently no summer RBL season due to the extreme Florida heat in the afternoons. I played in RBL one summer when they did have a season and the heat index often reached 100+ degrees. Not fun.

Originally, the league accepted players from Divisions 1 through 4. Currently, it is open to only Divisions 2, 3, and 4, along with any original players 'grandfathered in' from Division 1. Bill said there have also been a few players who moved from Division 4 down to Division 5 and they were also 'grandfathered in' because they still wanted to participate in the RBL.

According to its website the Restricted Bat League's goal is to have fun playing softball that is more like the game we all played when we were younger by:

- Making defense a more significant factor in the outcome of games.
- Allowing infielders and pitchers more time to react to a batted ball.
- Creating a safer game and extending the years that we can all play softball.

Arena League

Bob Baker, long-time commissioner for this league, who has played in it for 12 years, recently gave me a call. He said that the league is currently limited to Division II and the older (65+) Division I players. They generally have four teams in the summer season and seven teams during the fall and winter seasons. A sub list is maintained and players may move from that list to become full-time players, as the need and opportunity arises.

The Arena League plays its games at Sacks Field located just north of Rt. 466 off the Rolling Acres Road. The field is maintained by the Lady Lakes Park and Recreation Department, whose Director is Mike Burske. Bob told me that they do a great job of keeping the field in shape. Games are played on Monday mornings.

Bob said that players come primarily from The Villages® community, but also includes a few players from places like Ocala, Del Webb, and even Inverness.

I also recently talked with Terry Cole who started the league and who gave the league its name. The Arena league began about 14 years ago and consisted of several teams from throughout the area. According to Terry this included full teams from Ocala and Del Webb. The number of teams increased and then decreased over a few seasons; and eventually distilled down to a handful of teams like it is now.

Terry said that the original intent was to give the Division I and II players, who played in the Recreation

Leagues on Wednesdays and Fridays, another day (Monday) to play during the week.

As for the Arena League name, Terry explained it this way. "The field was smaller than those we had been playing on," Terry said. "When I looked at it, it kind of reminded me of the fields that the Arena League Football teams played on, which were smaller than a regular football field. So that was it. We called it the 'Arena League', a name which has stuck to this day."

You can use senior composite bats, but since the fence is only 250', if you hit a ball over the fence with one of those bats, you are out. Because of that rule, most players use a less lively 1.20 BPF, ASA-approved bat. You can hit home runs if you use those bats. The league maintains a list of the approved ASA bats.

Courtesy runners are allowed once a batter reaches base, whether it is a single, double, or triple. Bob said they don't keep stats and try to maintain it as "just a fun, overall league."

Bruce Forrester recently took over from Bob Baker as Commissioner of the Arena League.

Ladies Tri-County League

Avis Vaught was kind enough to provide the following information about this league:

"Tri-County Ladies Softball is a program for teams from the surrounding communities to compete in softball and to travel to various other softball complexes. The players must reside in the three counties of Lake,

Marion and Sumter. They play games twice a week. Teams participate at a skill level appropriate for their players in Divisions 1, 2, or 3. Each division has multiple teams to compete with during the season. The Villages has so many players that there are residents in all three divisions. The Tri-County program is played during the winter season, beginning in December and concluding with a week of championship games in the first two weeks of March.

This program provides an opportunity for our residents to be involved with the surrounding communities and to make new friends with others who share a common interest in playing the game of their childhood - our Nation's number one pastime game – softball."

Ladies Tournament Teams

I talked with Avis Vaught and she supplied me with this information. If you aspire to participate on a ladies travel team, there are numerous opportunities. Talk with Avis or just go to one of the Ladies Rec League games and you can find out how to get involved.

Tournament teams began in the late 1990's to represent the state of Florida and our community. The Tournament teams developed from The Villages® Recreation Softball Program. There was a mix of age group players participating. The Village Vixens, with Aileen Laing as manager, organized a team of age 55+ players.

In 2005, an influx of new residents with teaching and coaching skills had a big influence in developing more

Tournament (Travel) Teams. As The Vixens aged, a younger group of players formed the 50+ Silver Bullets, when the Vixens moved into the 60+ age class.

Teaching clinics provided an opportunity to teach the game and to improve player skills. This began to create more interest in the ladies recreation league; especially for players who had never had the opportunity to play as young girls. Today, many of these ladies, who were told when they were young that "you can't play because you are a girl," are still playing into their mid-seventies and eighties.

Midge Ferraro and her coaching staff created the Golden Gals Tournament Teams with 65 and 70 age brackets. Today, the Golden Gals includes 70, 75 and 80 age brackets; as well as the younger age groups - 55, 60 and 65 teams called The Players, who also play under Coach Ferraro.

The two most influential teams that were instrumental in creating the ladies tournament experience from The Villages® community and surrounding areas were the Village Vixens and The Golden Gals. There are also additional teams: Lightning, Village Diamonds, and Sunny Beaches that have provided opportunities for players to participate. There is a team in every age bracket for those who wish to continue their competitive tournament play past the age of 50.

There are organizations that sponsor tournaments in various parts of the country for Senior Softball and are involved with SSUSA, including the Florida Senior Games. Senior Games Nationals are held in odd years and World Senior Games held annually in Utah. See more information about this later in this chapter.

Tournament participation is very much a way of life with the softball ladies program here, along with the recreation leagues, senior games, and the Tri-County league. Many of our residents are happily active here in Florida, where they can play softball almost every day of the year. The future will continue to create opportunities for residents for competitive softball participation.

With softball in the Olympics and at the collegiate level, as well as organized K-12 competition for the girls, these young ladies will help the future of women's softball expand and they will one day be a part of Senior Ladies Softball.

Men's Travel Teams

Frenchie Le Tan has been one of the more active managers for Village travel teams, in particular the Frankie Brin sponsored teams since about 2008, and he provided me with much of this information.

There are certainly other managers and other teams, but I don't have the room or the time to cover them all. I just want to give the reader, who may be a newcomer that is interested in playing on a travel or tournament team, a basic idea of what may be involved. You can find out more precise information on all of the opportunities by asking around at the ball fields.

The local men's travel teams here actually belong to the Florida Half-Century League, which is made up of teams from throughout the state. There is a statewide governing body which administers everything and they generally have tournaments once a month, normally the second week, that feature two games on Saturday and two games on Sunday. Tournaments are held year-round.

These tournaments rotate playing at various venues in places like Lakeland, Fort Myers, Coral Gables, Sarasota, the Naples area, Bradenton, Winter Haven, the Tampa area, Winter Park, the Orlando area; and they also often play in The Villages® community a couple of times each year, around May and August in most years. When the local fields host a tournament, they are packed with spectators who flock to watch the quality teams and quality players from throughout the state.

The Half Century teams compete in age brackets, which are further broken down into groupings of players with similar skill levels. Age brackets start at 50-59, 60+, 65+, 70+, and 75+. Tournament groupings are set based upon past performance.

There are several travel teams made up of all Villagers or mostly Villagers. Many of the best players in our area play on these travel teams. A few people play on travel teams only. The teams are sponsored or have been sponsored by local businesses like Frankie Brin Financial, Beef O' Brady's, City Fire Restaurant, and Custom Apparel to name a few.

Sometimes these travel teams also compete in other tournaments throughout Florida which are separate from the Florida Half-Century League.

Frenchie said that there are over 220 teams in the Florida Half Century League and they are further divided into Districts. The local teams compete in District 4. He also told me that there are now a few teams in the league from South Georgia.

The various tournaments generally follow standard senior softball rules with the senior composite bats and such. Most of the tournaments require pitchers to use screens and runners can be substituted at any base. Occasionally, if there is a different rule or something for a particular tournament, it will be made known to the managers well ahead of time. Batters often start with a 1-1 ball/strike count in tournaments, as opposed to a standard 0-0 count, to speed up play.

A few local teams made up of top tier players travel to out-of-state tournaments, mostly in Georgia and South Carolina, but occasionally other states, too, including some in far away states. Parady Financial has sponsored some of these teams.

Occasionally you might encounter a 1 pitch, 30 minute limit tourney; or maybe a 2-2 count, 45 minute limit tournament. These are often set up because inclement weather conditions dictate a compressed schedule. .

Note - The Villages Recreation Department also usually sponsors at least one 'Open' tournament each fall. That's the one where in recent years the Canseco brothers, Ozzie and Jose, played; as well as former major league baseball star, Dante Bichette, and a number of former minor league and college players. Some local teams, such as the Frankie Brin 70's and Frankie Brin 74's, also participate. This tournament is not affiliated with the Florida Half Century League.

I think I have most of this information correct; but since I don't participate in Half Century or on any of the various travel teams, it is a little difficult to fully understand. Even Frenchie told me that it can get confusing.

But the bottom line is that there are very good players in this league and they travel frequently to weekend tournaments. Don't get too hung up on specifics in case I have gotten something wrong in this section. I just wanted you to be aware of this league and the travel teams. If you aspire to participate at this level, you can get more information from Frenchie Le Tan, Frankie Murth, or any number of other local players and managers. Just ask around.

Veterans/Military Tournaments

AUTHOR'S NOTE: Since these tournaments are not part of a regular league, and since some of the long-time coordinators have dropped out, along with various other changes that have been made, it was initially a little difficult to track down accurate information. But thanks to Ted Ramirez, Bob Nyce, Bob Hrabak, Karen Coll, Joe Rocco, and Pam Napoletano, I was able to get some information. I have written it to the best of my knowledge from discussions with these folks. If I have inadvertently gotten something wrong, I apologize.

The main point is that there have been three separate veterans tournaments held in recent years and many of those involved hope to continue them. Check around, if you are interested, and you can find out more.

Remember, as one Recreation Department official recently told me, everything is fluid and subject to change from season to season and from year to year. All players agree, though, that Danny Jacobs and his staff work really hard to help put on quality Veterans Tournaments when requested. This is a very Veteran friendly community with a high percentage of former military vets. And many of them play softball!

These annual tournaments are intended to honor military veterans; to let them play softball and enjoy the camaraderie of fellow teammate veterans from the same service branches; and to let them compete for 'bragging rights' that last until the next year. This makes for some good competition and also for some good-natured ribbing among the military branches. There are presently three concurrent tournaments held each fall that are played at Saddlebrook and Buffalo Glen on Sundays in November.

One tournament is comprised of teams formed by combining Division 1, 2, and 3 players; one is strictly for Division 4 players; while the other tournament is comprised of teams formed by combining Division 5, K5, and ladies players, who have been included on the D5/K5 team for several years now.

Ted Ramirez was involved with the Veteran's/Military Tournament for years. He recently told me that he organized the combined Division 1/2/3 tourney from 2003 – 2017. It actually began in 2002 with Pete Cooper leading it, but Pete moved away and Ted took it over.

The Division 4/5 teams played together for several years until splitting into two separate tournaments a few years ago. Jerry May was the first coordinator, while others including Bob Hrabak and Joe Rocco have since been involved.

Everyone says that these have always been great tournaments, enjoyed by the players, who are all veterans that play softball here in The Villages® community. The tournaments include players who have been evaluated for play in their respective Divisions. If you are a veteran who has never played softball here, you are not eligible to play in these tournaments. You must go through an evaluation process.

Ted said that these tournaments were originally held on the Sunday nearest Memorial Day, but after a couple of years with really hot weekends, the decision was made to move them to November, as close to Veterans Day as possible. The tournaments were initially held at the Saddlebrook fields. Once Buffalo Glen opened up in 2007, both complexes were used.

One year a Division will hold all of its games at Buffalo Glen and the other Divisions will play games at Saddlebrook. Then, they alternate the locations the following year, and on and on.

In the early years Ted said that he would solicit applications from players, select the managers, form teams, and try to keep the skill levels as close as possible. Of course, he had to make sure he got pitchers assigned to each team. In recent years the teams have been formed through more of a 'draft' system from among the applicants.

After things got rolling, Ted said that there would normally be about 10 teams in his tournament. The last couple of years of his leadership there were: 5 Army teams; 2 Air Force teams; 2 Navy teams; and a combined Marine/Coast Guard team.

Bob Hrabak said that he managed the Marine team in his tournament for 9 years. In the early years he said that there were usually six teams participating, but that since about 2014 there have been 10-12 teams in the Division 4 Tourney. In one recent year he recalled that there were six Army teams; three Navy teams; two from the Air Force; and one combined Marine/Coast Guard squad.

Joe Rocco told me that the 2019 Division 5/K5/Ladies Veterans Tournament included 3 Army teams, 1 Marine team, 1 Air Force team, 2 combined Navy/Coast Guard teams, and one ladies team. This tournament has had between 8 and 14 teams represented in various years. The ladies, who won the 2019 tournament, represent all branches of the military on their team.

Pam Napoletano sent me the following information about the ladies' participation: "In 2012 we entered the first all-women's team in the Veterans Tournament. In

2013 we won our first game in that tourney. By 2018 we made it to the championship game, but lost. In 2019 we won the D5 championship of the Thomas E. Kennedy Memorial Veterans Day Tournament."

And Karen Coll added: "I've played in this tournament for four years, the last two as manager. We had nine Army veterans; five from the Air Force; and one Navy veteran on last year's winning team. They are an amazing group of women from all types of military positions, who served our great country," she said.

Coll went on to name the following team members from that 2019 team: Sharie Russell; Eugenia Ulman; Deb McCarty; Pam Napoletano; Lori Bond; Jodi Pritchard; Terry Thomas; Carol Waters; Paulette Saffle; Heath Davenport; Hope Alger; Donna Wright; Angie Poole; Annette McMillan; and, of course, Karen Coll.

I believe that all of the military tournaments began as double elimination. Of course, it took two back-to-back Sundays to complete all the games and some teams had to play multiple games on the final day. Because of this, I understand that the Veterans Tournaments are all now single elimination with a loser's bracket, which guarantees each team to play at least two games; but not so many games as in a double elimination tournament.

You may want to check that out, if you're interested, but I guess it doesn't really matter. In any case, there are Vet tournaments that you can play in, unless interest wanes. It takes a lot of effort and commitment from the organizers and coordinators to put on these tournaments. I was told there was one year that the Division 1/2/3 tournament was not played.

I played in two or three of the D1/2/3 tournaments from about 2015-2018 and I thoroughly enjoyed playing in those tournaments. I played on an Air Force team one year that advanced to the finals undefeated through the winner's bracket, only to lose twice to a strong Army team that we had defeated earlier in the tournament.

The tournaments have all kicked off with a military style opening ceremony, which introduces and recognizes the various branches; and the teams generally line the fields, along the base paths. There is a Pledge of Allegiance; a patriotic song or other music; and honor guards from the American Legion, VFW, or the Villages Marine Honor Guard march out and display the colors.

Local singer and softball player Larry Rivellese has often sung the National Anthem; Billy Leeper also sang the National Anthem at a recent D5 tournament. Some years Dave Czohara, who played trumpet in the Navy Band during his service years, plays Taps. In last year's D5 tournament, there was a tape which played the official military songs of each of the five service branches.

Invited officials have often attended, including Col. Adderly, a pilot from MacDill Air Force Base in Tampa, who threw out the first pitch for the D1/2/3 tournament in 2017.

Village resident Leo Champagne, a Marine veteran who participated in the historic flag raising at Iwo Jima in World War II, threw out the first pitch of the D4/5 tourney for many years.

Harry Brady a World War II veteran of the Battle of Okinawa was a special guest honoree at one of the D5 tourneys; and one of the players, Wayne Lotsberg, a decorated naval aviator during Vietnam, threw out the first pitch to open the tournament.

Bob Nyce has been involved in helping organize things for the D1/2/3 tourney the past couple of years. Others helping him have included: Mark Hildebrand, Vernon Brooks, John Wyks, Darren Ivey, Larry Wizauer, Darrell Smith, Don Mullenix, and Rick Fredieu.

Plans are a little uncertain regarding the 2020 tourneys due to the corona virus situation and various other factors, but I suspect they will continue in some form because of the large contingent of military veterans who play softball in The Villages® community. If you are interested in these tournaments, you will want to check with some of those folks mentioned, or with the Recreation Department, for the latest information.

Senior Games

I won't get too deep into this topic, but I did want to let newcomers know that there is something called the Senior Games for 50+ age athletes. It began in the early 1990's and involves every state in the country.

Each state holds regional games for team and individual activities. Top finishers may then participate in the

State Games Championships, an annual event that can qualify them to participate in the Senior Games Nationals (also known as Senior Olympics.) These are held on the odd numbered years.

Senior Games sports include just about anything imaginable – track & field; paddle sports; swimming; basketball; archery; billiards; and much, much more, including, of course, softball.

Both men's and women's softball teams from this community participate in the Florida Senior Games. Age brackets start at 50+ and also include brackets for every five year group beyond that, i.e. 55+, 60+, 65+, etc.

The residents who participate are involved either on a travel team, tournament team, or recreational league team within their respective age bracket. Anyone can participate and is welcome to be involved as a player, team assistant, or a volunteer.

The Villages® community hosts the Regional Games in the spring (usually April). State Championships are traditionally held in August for softball teams and December for all other sport activities. The Villages® Recreation Department is very involved with assisting and supporting residents with their Senior Games activities.

You can check it out and gather more information if you think you might be interested.

V. APPENDIX

Player Bios

Following are the player Bio's for both the men's and women's leagues. Many of these men and ladies play in more than one league; some play 5 or even 6 days a week. Others may play just one or two days a week.

Of course, with about 3,000 softball players in The Villages® community, it would be nearly impossible to mention all of them in a short book like this. I've tried to include a sample of players from all of the leagues and divisions, as well as travel teams. There are over 125 players featured in this Bio Section. I have listed the men players and the women players in separate sections; and alphabetically.

The point of this part of the book is to provide the reader with a cross-section of players from every league and skill level to give you an idea of:

- Where they were born and where they moved here from;
- What positions they play and what leagues/ divisions they play in;
- What were their jobs and careers prior to moving here;
- Their ages, if they were willing to say;
- How many years they have played softball here, as well as throughout their lives;
- What others sports they have been involved with over the years;

- Their personal observations of the softball scene locally;
- Significant individual players, managers, and others whom they have known;
- Various general comments.

I distributed questionnaires randomly, particularly in leagues where I did not play. Of course, when push came to shove, in order to get enough players listed in this section, I did ask various friends and teammates to help me out. Other players heard about this book and also asked me to be included. The whole point of this section, though, is to provide the reader with a cross-section of players; not all of the best players in each league or anything like that, although many of those listed certainly are.

I want the reader and those new to The Villages® community to get a sense of the overall participation and a sense of who all is playing softball here. You newcomers who are reading this book may also soon want to join the ranks of the players mentioned in this section.

*   *   *   *   *

Since I asked so many players to share their Bio information for this section, I guess it's only fair for me to do the same. Here goes:

Dan Kincaid, age 70, and born in Frank, WV (and yes, that's the name of the town, not my father's name. We have some really small towns over there in the beautiful Mountain State.) We moved here from Athens, OH. I was a forester, who retired after 31 years with the U.S.

Forest Service, primarily working at various national forest locations in five states, as well as temporary assignments in several others. I've played softball here since 2014.

I've played in several leagues: R4, R3, R2, N3, CFL, 68+, and RBL since I began in 2014. I also played in the Veterans/Military tournament a couple of times, on the Air Force team. And believe it or not, I've actually played every position on the field, some of them probably not so well. Most of this was out of necessity due to a player being absent. I have even pitched twice; although not very well either time (I walked too many batters.) But my primary position and the one I play best is first base.

Two years ago I was trying to figure out what all positions I had played since I arrived here. The only one I had not played was shortstop. I told my manager at the time, Lindell Grigg, and he said he would have me play SS for an inning some game. Well, he did, and I actually stayed there for three innings. Luckily, I didn't get a lot of action.

My sports background in high school was baseball, football, and basketball (we won a state championship my junior year and I was named captain my senior season.) I played youth baseball from the Pee Wee League, through Little League, Babe Ruth, Senior Babe Ruth, and American Legion. I also played a few seasons of adult amateur baseball in Huntington, WV and Columbus, OH.

I played college baseball, starting in left field on the freshman team, before a promising career (at least I was hoping for that) was derailed by a serious shoulder injury the spring before my sophomore year. Despite fairly intense rehab, it never healed properly and during my junior season, I called it quits. Several years later, I began playing fast pitch softball (for two summers) and then slow pitch. During my 30s, I played quite a bit of slow pitch softball, mostly in Ohio, including in leagues and on traveling tournament teams. By age 39 or so, I was done until I moved here.

I also played in several adult basketball leagues throughout my 20s, 30s, and until age 40. For most of my life my other primary sports were outdoor things, like hunting, fishing, hiking, camping, canoeing, and so forth. I shoot some pool (billiards) here, play a little platform tennis, and try to play golf at least twice a year whether I want to or not (it's not my thing; you should watch the funny Robin Williams skit on You Tube about how and why the Scottish people invented golf.) Mostly now, for me, it's softball and writing books; this is #11.

The softball here is fantastic – the fields, the way it is organized, the competition, the players and managers, the support people, and really, everything. And it's year round! It's the best I've been around and from talking with other players, they all feel the same way. For many of them, this is the main reason they moved here.

The players are too numerous to mention, but it seems like I've been on a lot of teams with Dave Williams, Vernon Brooks, and Ray Saberg, three good players. The managers and assistant managers I've played for have all been outstanding – Rick Valdes, Vernon Brooks, Wally Dias, Al Deibler, John Cilento, Billy Taylor, Dan List, Dana Lambillotte, Darren Ivey, Sal Riggio, Jim Cantalupo, Bob Alan, Dave Williams, Woody Wood, Jack Marx, Larry Thomas, Steve Mols, Don Glennan, Steve Barton, Jack Nesci, Ken Scanlon, Bob Cronin, Lindell Grigg, John Veltre, Ernie Joyal, Ron Guba, John Ashby, Walter Banko, Ed Krisha, and I'm sure I've missed a couple of others - my apologies; no slight intended.

That's about it for me. I encourage all of you who are thinking about playing softball here to go for it. I don't think you'll regret it.

As I begin the player listings in this section, I want to personally thank all of those who contributed. It has been my privilege to talk with you and to get to know your background, as well as learn about your passion for playing softball. Thank you for sharing.

When players mention The Villages in their Bio responses in this section, they are referring to The Villages® community. There is no affiliation with, or sponsorship by, Holding Company of The Villages or its affiliated entities.

Now for the player Bio's (these were mostly all returned to me between January and May of 2020):

SOFTBALL IN THE VILLAGES® COMMUNITY

(Men's Player Bio's - Alphabetical List)

Name/Age – Bob Alan, 72

Where Born? – Cleveland, OH

Moved here from? – Phoenix, AZ

Job(s), Career – TV Meteorologist

Leagues & Divisions played in – Neighborhood 4, Rec. 3, 68+, RBL

Years Played – In The Villages -2; in life - 50

Positions/Roles – P, 1B, 2B, 3B, Co-Manager

Softball/Baseball/Other Sports Background - Basketball, baseball, golf, tennis

Thoughts on softball here – I love the competition, fellowship, and camaraderie. This is a great environment for softball and other recreation.

Key players, teammates, & others important to you – Dave Williams, Jack Nagle, Dan Kincaid, Lindell Grigg, Jim Holloway, and many more!

Other comments – I love the softball environment here, the maintenance of the facilities, and I've made some of the best friendships ever.

Name/Age – Roger Anderson, 75

Where Born? – Colorado, but grew up in Elko, NV

Moved here from? - Arkansas

Job(s), Career – Physician, MD

Leagues & Divisions played in – N4, R4, 68+, RBL

Years Played – August 2012 to present

Positions/Roles - Outfield

Softball/Baseball/Other Sports Background – HS football, baseball, basketball; recreational tennis. Did not play baseball or softball for 45 years prior to moving to The Villages.

Thoughts on softball here – I've enjoyed Neighborhood ball the most – less stress.

Key players, teammates, & others important to you – Norm Purvis

Other comments – I had never played slow pitch softball and learning not to swing at the trajectory of the pitch took practice.

Name/Age – Art Anton, 69

Where Born? - Cuba

Moved here from? – NW suburb of Chicago

Job(s), Career – AT&T Outside Plant Technician

Leagues & Divisions played in – R3/N3/CFL/68+ and RBL

Years Played – 2015 to present

Positions/Roles – OF, IF, Umpire

Softball/Baseball/Other Sports Background -HS football, basketball, baseball/college football/softball and flag football leagues.

Thoughts on softball here – Moved here for the golf courses in retirement. When I saw firsthand the softball operation, I was sold on that, too!

Key players, teammates, & others important to you – Gil Kettelhut was the 1st Mgr that I played for – good organizational and communications skills. Played with Ev Arnold, in his mid 80s and still competing. Ron Nikstad and Mariano Ramos are two of the better hitters I have played with.

Other comments – I've developed friendships with players from all over the country and Canada. New teammates each season keeps it interesting and fresh. If you can't find an activity you enjoy in this community, then you're not trying!

Name/Age – Bob Baker, 72

Where Born? – Fort Dodge, IA
Moved here from? – Gonzales, LA
Job(s), Career – Graduated Iowa State University 1970 Aerospace Engineering; career start w/Fisher Controls, a company manufacturing instruments & valves for process industries such as power, oil & gas, chemical & petrochemical, etc.; transferred to Boston area as one of its independent sales representatives. Late 1970's career change via buying into family farm corporation and moving back to Iowa; 14 years farming and then major split with family, so rejoined Fisher Controls in process control industry. Multiple positions in marketing & management at Fisher Controls, ultimately being Director of North American sales and managing 32 independent sales representative corporations. Hired in 2000 by John H Carter Company as Vice President (one of the independent sales corps noted above, headquartered in New Orleans); friends told us about The Villages in 2004 so immediately checked it out & built 1st home here in that year. Retired 2006 and now in 2nd home here.

Leagues & Divisions played in – Evaluated as a "1" but initially played in Rec 2, then moved into Rec 1; also Arena League. On Florida Half Century travel teams over the years for Talon Financial, Beef O'Brady, Frankie Brin Financial, and TD Financial; played age brackets, starting at 60+, then 65+ and 70+.
Years Played – 3 seasons per year in The Villages for 14 years, missing 3-4 seasons due to injury or shoulder surgeries.

Positions/Roles – 3B, SF, P, scorekeeper, manager in D2 for a couple seasons; Manager in Arena League & Commissioner for 10 years – retired in 2020.

Softball/Baseball/Other Sports Background – Played several years in the 1980's & early 1990's on 16" slow pitch teams in Iowa, both in league play and on travel teams. High school played football (QB), basketball (F), and track (discus, 440 relay, 880, 2 mile relay). Heart condition discovered ended HS football senior year so when attending Iowa State University, stayed close to football via equipment manager for 4 years (notable head coach & assistants were Johnny Majors, Jimmy Johnson, Jackie Sherrill).

Thoughts on softball here – Best there is!! Well managed with opportunities for all skill levels; top notch fields/complexes as compared to many travel team tournament venues. Having 3 seasons with drafts each season allows one to play with and get to know hundreds of individuals over a career.

Key players, teammates, or other important individuals you've known here - Dan List (passed 2019) was one of first individuals I met as he was returning to softball after stem cell replacement. Tremendous individual, manager, competitor and a huge inspiration. Dave Black (retired from softball several years ago) has always been a friend and confidant. Actually, the list is too long to mention, having met a huge number of individuals through softball.

Name/Age – Walter Banko, 72

Where Born? – Mt. Pleasant, PA; grew up in Scottdale, PA

Moved here from? – Loveland, OH

Job(s), Career – Veterans Administration; and COO for Network 10 in OH

Leagues & Divisions played in – R3, 68+, CFL

Years Played – 8 yrs.

Positions/Roles – All IF & OF positions; Mgr. 68+

Softball/Baseball/Other Sports Background – Baseball to age 15; fast pitch softball 2 yrs during college

Thoughts on softball here – Softball here is a great experience. The more you play, the more friends you make. Great exercise and social activity.

Key players, teammates, & others important to you - Hard question; many good players here.

Other comments – The more you play, and with different teams, offers an opportunity to meet and get to know people you would never know otherwise. Also, helps you recall your baseball life growing up that was set aside during your work years.

Name/Age – Mark Beasley, 67

Where Born? – Granite City, IL

Moved here from? – Glen Carbon, IL

Job(s), Career – 43 years – U.S. Steel

Leagues & Divisions played in – R2, R3, RBL, CFL, 68+

Years Played – 3 yrs.

Positions/Roles – LF, 2B, RF, SS, C

Softball/Baseball/Other Sports Background – Softball, baseball, soccer, basketball, personal trainer for 8 yrs., fitness instructor

Thoughts on softball here – Awesome program

Key players, teammates, & others important to you – Lindell Grigg introduced me to the program; Bob Wielenga moved me to shortstop, where I had never played and I've been playing there ever since.

Other comments – Enjoyed playing for Manager Bob Wielenga the most. The camaraderie among the guys is great for the most part.

Name/Age – Jeff Bekasi, 70

Where Born? – Torrington, CT

Moved here from? – Harleysville, PA

Job(s), Career – Service Center Mgr/ Repair Operations Mgr/ Product Mgr for Process Control Equipment Manufacturer.

Leagues & Divisions played in – CFL, N3, R3
Years Played – 11
Positions/Roles – OF, P, 1B, Manager

Softball/Baseball/Other Sports Background – HS soccer, baseball, basketball; freshman soccer and baseball at UConn; 1 yr varsity baseball at UConn; company softball and basketball teams.

Thoughts on softball here – Having grown up playing team sports, playing softball in The Villages provides that same camaraderie and those friendships. Lots of fun!

Key players, teammates, & others important to you – Many great players and teammates, but Tom McGann took me under his wing and we have been good friends ever since.

Other comments – Many new people talk about "tryouts." I tell them that it is not a tryout, but an evaluation, so that they can put you in a league with your similar skill level. But everyone who wants to play softball will get to play softball.

Name/Age – Dave Bigelow, 74

Where Born? – Lansing, MI

Moved here from? – Lansing, MI

Job(s), Career – Dealership – Service Director

Leagues & Divisions played in – R4, N4, Central Florida

Years Played - 14

Positions/Roles – P, Commissioner N4 for 7 ½ years; presently President of R4.

Softball/Baseball/Other Sports Background – Played some slow pitch towards the end of my working years. Started playing co-ed slow pitch after I retired.

Thoughts on softball here – Whoever thought at our ages we would still be playing competitive softball? Only in The Villages would you ever find such a well organized program.

Key players, teammates, & others important to you – Have met and become friends with so many super nice and caring people from all walks of life.

Other comments – Dan, good luck with the book.

Name/Age – Tom Bortle, 62

Where Born? – Albany, NY

Moved here from? – Colonie, NY

Job(s), Career –Public Safety Communications/9-1-1

Leagues & Divisions played in – R3, N3, CFL

Years Played – 7 ½ years

Positions/Roles – SF, IF, P/Manager/CFL Board

Softball/Baseball/Other Sports Background – Avid golfer and bowler; softball in late 1990s in various fun leagues

Thoughts on softball here – Some of the best softball complexes anywhere; well organized and well run leagues; camaraderie among players is a joy.

Key players, teammates, & others important to you – My first manager in N3 was Bryan Johnson. He was a mentor, showing how to have fun and enjoy softball here. He coached the Bonnybrook/Lynnhaven team that I played for.

Other comments – Many players and many friendships have become a part of my 'retirement life.'

Name/Age – John Breck, 85

Where Born? – Iowa

Moved here from? – Davenport, Iowa

Job(s), Career – High School Teacher

Leagues & Divisions played in – Divisions 1 - 5
Years Played – 23
Positions/Roles –Infield, Catcher

Softball/Baseball/Other Sports Background -
Golf, Water Volleyball, Sand Volleyball

Thoughts on softball here – We came for a visit and
when I saw players at Knudson Field, I told my wife
"this is where I want to live." I have known and seen
tremendous growth in softball here – from 8 teams in 2
divisions..... and now I don't even know where one of
the complexes is located!

**Key players, teammates, & others important to
you** – Most of the players that I started with are now
playing in heaven. There are only two players that I can
think of who are still playing from when I started – Ron
Dungan and Bob LaFlamme.

Other comments – I believe that I am now one of the
five oldest guys still playing. I think I am the oldest
manager and the one who has been managing the
longest. I have witnessed two players hit four home
runs over the fence in one game – John Riccutto and
George Rodriguez, both still living.

Name/Age – Vernon Brooks, 77

Where Born? – Ellisville, Mississippi

Moved here from? – Richmond, VA

Job(s), Career – VP Equipment Leasing/Finance

Leagues & Divisions played in – Rec 3, N3, CFL, Classic 70, Military/Veteran Tourneys, Travel team

Years Played – 2010 to present
Positions/Roles – SS, 2B, SF, Manager

Softball/Baseball/Other Sports Background-HS baseball, church softball, US Air Force softball, fast pitch softball for 12 years, slow pitch since then. Played against 'The King and His Court' in 1968 and 1971. Once played on a travel team in TN sponsored by Elvis Presley, though we never saw him personally. Played competitive tennis in VA with USTA 4.5 rating.

Thoughts on softball here – Some of the best fields and age-group players I've ever seen. Very well organized.

Key players, teammates, & others important to you – All players have been 'key' in my eyes. My summer '16 Dolphins team went 19-2 to finish first in R3 and then won the tourney. Great memory!

Other comments – Feel blessed to play this 'kids' game at this stage of my life. I've made so many good friends here. It helps keep me going from day to day.

Name/Age – John P. Cahill, Jr., 70

Where Born? – Upstate NY

Moved here from? – Central GA

Job(s), Career – Retired Air Force officer 32 yrs., Defense Contractor 10 yrs.

Leagues & Divisions played in – R1, Classics, Arena, N1/2   **Years Played** – 5 yrs.

Positions/Roles – All positions, ump, scorekeeper

Softball/Baseball/Other Sports Background – Little League and American Legion baseball, HS football, basketball, baseball; military softball, flag football, volleyball, basketball; civilian softball and basketball; coached fast pitch and slow pitch softball.

Thoughts on softball here – Great experience. One of the top three sports here. Well organized, competitive, available to all levels and ages. Travel teams here are among the best in FL and the whole southeast. Great camaraderie.

Key players, teammates, & others important to you – Dave Norval, Hank Culley, Doug Goslee, Donny Meyer, Dave McDermott, Greg Hanson, Billy Warble, Ollie Schniederjans, Bud Shelley, Dave Sellars, Eddie Connell, Steve Wilson, Bill Devine, Charlie Wilson, Bill DiCarlo, Bob Baker, Bill Cecil, Bob Fritsch.

Name/Age – Bob Campbell, 72

Where Born? – Troy, NY

Moved here from? – Rensselaer, NY

Job(s), Career – Computer Room Supervisor for different agencies with the State of New York

Leagues & Divisions played in – R4, R5, N4, N5

Years Played - 13

Positions/Roles – 3B, SS, SF, manager

Softball/Baseball/Other Sports Background - Little League, Babe Ruth, & American Legion baseball; softball—fast pitch, medium pitch, Big Ball, High Arc

Thoughts on softball here – The fields are great!

Key players, teammates, & others important to you – Teammates and Managers - Randy Aguiar, Roy Dugan, Remo Florio, Pat Passaretti, Ron Coen, Bud Kirchens, Jim Lyall, Alan Richardson, Bob Laflamme, Tom Heffner, Jim Garry, John Horwath, Vince Curran, Dom Gualtieri

Other comments – Used to get better newspaper coverage and some games televised on VNN. Wish we could get back to that level of coverage.

Name/Age – Jim Cantalupo, 68

Where Born? – Astoria/Queens, NY

Moved here from? – Long Island, NY - 2010

Job(s), Career – CPA on Wall Street for 32 years

Leagues & Divisions played in – N3, RBL

Years Played – 2010 to present

Positions/Roles – SF, Rover (I would like to think I play the position very different than others.)

Softball/Baseball/Other Sports Background – Youth baseball, high school, one year in college, then industrial league softball till age 40.

Thoughts on softball here – One of the main reasons I retired here; fantastic/competitive/fair

Key players, teammates, & others important to you – Buttonwood N3 team won 23 straight games in 2014-2015; co-manage RBL team with Woody Wood. Many great volunteers involved.

Other comments – When we're between the lines we feel like kids again. Have made many lifelong friends. Thanks to all who help us maintain a high level of play on great fields.

Name/Age – Fred Caprio, 75

Where Born? – Hoboken, NJ

Moved here from? – Colonia, NJ

Job(s), Career – Over the years, maintenance, deck building, roofing. Retired from the NY/NJ Port Authority as Head of Maintenance for the World Trade Center in New York City.

Leagues & Divisions played in – N4, R4, 68+

Years Played – 11 years

Positions/Roles – 2B, OF, P, C

Softball/Baseball/Other Sports Background – Competitive billiards; golf as fun.

Thoughts on softball here – Great place to play softball at any age. Have made a lot of good friends.

Key players, teammates, & others important to you – Too many to mention by name..........at my age names don't come easy.

Other comments – Here in The Villages, softball, billiards, and golf keep me active and off the couch. There are many activities here to help us live a better life.

Name/Age – Milt Casablanca, 71

Where Born? – Brooklyn, NY

Moved here from? – Center Moriches, NY

Job(s), Career-Insurance Claims & Marketing; Agent

Leagues & Divisions played in – R2,R3,N2,N3,68+

Years Played – Since 2010, with one year off

Positions/Roles – SS when younger; OF in Villages

Softball/Baseball/Other Sports Background - Divisions 1,2,3 softball on Long Island

Thoughts on softball here – Great program and players who have become great friends.

Key players, teammates, & others important to you – Many, but I will mention: Len Griffin, Tom McGann, Bob Nizlek, Dave Pope, Dave Williams, Gary Roth, Jim Holloway, Pat Rice, Ray Saberg, Dennis Bauch, Hap Hazard, Roger Duncan, and Dan Callahan.

Other comments – In 2014 I was diagnosed with pancreatic cancer on Long Island. The day before surgery I decided to play one last game against the NY Streaks. Afterward, those players lined up to hug me and wish me well. It was very touching; I'll never forget it. It's why I love softball and cherish my teammates!

Name/Age – Don Chambers, 64

Where Born? – Corning, NY

Moved here from? – Lehigh Valley, PA

Job(s), Career – College Professor in Finance

Leagues & Divisions played in – N3, Rec 3, RBL

Years Played - 4

Positions/Roles - Shortstop

Softball/Baseball/Other Sports Background – High school and college swimming

Thoughts on softball here – Those running things have a passion, for not only the game of softball, but also for the people who play the game.

Key players, teammates, & others important to you – The volunteers who oversee Div 3 softball – the Board, umpires, score keepers – deserve credit for the program's success.

Other comments – The leadership pursues parity and sportsmanship, which enhances the fun and camaraderie of playing softball together in retirement.

Name/Age – John Cilento, 72

Where Born? – Brooklyn, NY

Moved here from? – Port Washington, NY

Job(s), Career – Financial Services industry – Worked in credit depts. of large bank-owned factoring companies analyzing financial statements to decide credit worthiness.

Leagues & Divisions played in – R4, N4, 68+

Years Played – Since 2012

Positions/Roles – P, 1B, 2B, manager

Softball/Baseball/Other Sports Background – Brooklyn streets and schoolyards on Sunday afternoons (after a big Italian dinner) – baseball (my father and uncle would pitch to the neighborhood kids after church), softball, football, basketball, hockey, as well as punch ball, stoop ball, and stickball, using a pink rubber Spaldeen ball. We played a little golf, but not much due to the expense. Those times were very important to me and taught us many life lessons.

Thoughts on softball here – It has given us a great chance to continue playing ball at this age. The leagues and fields are top notch. The friendships with teammates and competitors are truly special.

Key players, teammates, & others important to you – Many truly amazing people. Rick Valdes, a fellow manager and dear friend, gave me sound advice about managing: it's not always about winning; how we should conduct ourselves; lead by example; and remember that everyone is trying his best.

Bob Tambellini is a great player, teammate, and close friend – he has a quiet, positive attitude and sometimes helps cool my hot Sicilian temper.

Other comments – Playing softball here has re-opened an avenue in my life that I thought was lost. I never thought that I'd be more active today than when I was younger – softball and golf every week, coupled with all of the other activities that are available here, there is no time to be idle! This is truly Disneyland for adults. I treasure every day.

Name/Age – Charles Clare, 63

Where Born? – Connecticut

Moved here from? - Virginia

Job(s), Career – Dept. of State; and U.S. Air Force

Leagues & Divisions played in – R2, N1/2, Arena, RBL, CFL, Military Veterans Tournaments

Years Played - 5

Positions/Roles – OF, P

Softball/Baseball/Other Sports Background – HS baseball - shortstop

Thoughts on softball here – It's like I found paradise!

Key players, teammates, & others important to you – There's a great group of guys in every league I play in.

Other comments – I never thought in my wildest dreams that I would be playing softball at my age - six times a week, year round. I play roughly 205 games a year. I'll slow down when I'm dead.

Name/Age – Terry Cole, 77

Where Born? – Winter Haven, FL

Moved here from? – Winter Haven, FL

Job(s), Career – Owned my own business. Sold it in 1996 to resume playing softball in this area.

Leagues & Divisions played in – Can't remember all of the travel and tournament teams. Have played in R1, R2, R4, R5, N1, N2, N3, N4, and N5. I helped start the 68+ League and the Arena League.

Years Played – 20+ yrs locally
Positions/Roles – OF, P, SF

Softball/Baseball/Other Sports Background - Softball since grade school.

Thoughts on softball here – Softball here has to be the best and largest of any retirement community anywhere. That's what attracted me to move here.

Key players, teammates, & others important to you – I most admired and enjoyed playing with Mike Christy on his 3 Amigo's teams. He sponsored travel teams that I played on. He owned the local bowling pro shop.

Other comments – To be 77 years old and still playing competitive softball is beyond anything I could have ever imagined. My only regret is that I won't make it another 77 years.

Name/Age – Jim Creed, 69

Where Born? – Leominster, MA

Moved here from? – Leominster, MA

Job(s), Career – Learning Disabilities Specialist

Leagues & Divisions played in – Arena, CFL, RBL, R2, N2, Half-Century

Years Played – 2010 - present

Positions/Roles – OF, umpire, scorekeeper

Softball/Baseball/Other Sports Background – Played one year of college basketball; coached HS football and baseball

Thoughts on softball here – Excellent facilities and organization. D2 has had excellent leadership and volunteers, which makes it an enjoyable experience for all.

Key players, teammates, & others important to you – Dan List was a special individual both as a player and manager. I felt privileged to be chosen by him in my first season.

Other comments – Softball here is both an athletic and a social success.

Name/Age – Dave Czohara, 68

Where Born? – Springfield, MA

Moved here from? – Cooper City, FL

Job(s), Career – Musician – trumpet; played in Navy Band 1970-92; been freelancing steadily since; played on a Grammy Award album in 1995.

Leagues & Divisions played in – R3, R4, N3, N4, CFL, and 68+; plays trumpet for Veterans Tourneys

Years Played – 2006 to present

Positions/Roles – OF, SF, Manager-N, umpire

Softball/Baseball/Other Sports Background – Baseball – Little League thru high school, hockey

Thoughts on softball here – The best experience possible. I enjoy the concept of being on different teams three times a year. Being around guys and gals who want to compete and show sportsmanship is great.

Key players, teammates, & others important to you – Chuck Bowman-Div.3, CFL; Frank Horanzy-Div.4; Bud McFarland-Div.4, 68+; Rick Montroy-Div.3/4.

Other comments – I appreciate all the volunteers, umpires, and scorers. Playing the game at this age is a gift.

Name/Age – Lou Daigle, 67

Where Born? – Connecticut (CT)

Moved here from? – CT, but still 'snowbirding'

Job(s), Career – Retired from United Technologies; worked on the Space Shuttle & the Int'l Space Station programs.

Leagues & Divisions played in – Rec. 3, RBL, 68+, and Neighborhood 3.

Years Played - 10

Positions/Roles - Outfield

Softball/Baseball/Other Sports Background – Played baseball in youth until high school graduation.

Thoughts on softball here – Various leagues are well run. We're fortunate to have these fields and facilities.

Key players, teammates, & others important to you – Many wonderful and talented people. Steve Greenberg, manager of the Rec 3 Ravens team, has been a sort of 'mentor' to me.

Other comments – Never thought I'd be playing softball at this age. I'm fortunate to be physically able to play. It's tremendous fun; there are many nice people.

Name/Age – Floyd Davis, 72

Where Born? – Miami, FL

Moved here from? – Miami, FL

Job(s), Career – Director of Purchasing for Hilton Hotels

Leagues & Divisions played in – R4, RBL, 68+, N4

Years Played - 8

Positions/Roles – OF, IF

Softball/Baseball/Other Sports Background – Baseball, football, softball (fast pitch, medium pitch, and slow pitch). I also love to bowl.

Thoughts on softball here– It's a great thing.

Key players, teammates, & others important to you – All softball players that I've come in contact with have been great individuals.

Other comments - Whoever thought when you retired, you would be playing competitive softball again? **AUTHOR'S NOTE** – Floyd is an accomplished bowler who regularly competes in local tournaments and does very well.

Name/Age – Wally Dias, 73

Where Born? – Fall River, MA

Moved here from? – Rhode Island

Job(s), Career – Manager, Prudential Insurance

Leagues & Divisions played in – R3, R4, N3, CFL

Years Played – 2004 - 2019

Positions/Roles – P, Manager; Board member and President R3 and N3 for 10+ years. Still makes schedules for three leagues.

Softball/Baseball/Sports Background - None

Thoughts on softball here – The best programs available anywhere; players from all levels can find their comfort zone.

Key players, teammates, & others important to you – Too numerous to mention, but the best part is the association with the players. All the volunteers-umpires, Board, scorers, managers.

Other comments – *Author's note*: According to the R3 website, Wally still holds the best won/loss record (.611) for managers with eight or more seasons. Wally managed for 22 seasons and I was fortunate to play for him two or three times on the Chiefs. Great manager! Great person!

Name/Age – Bill DiCarlo, 64

Where Born? – Long Island, NY

Moved here from? – Hong Kong

Job(s), Career – Stadium/Arena/Convention Center Director

Leagues & Divisions played in – R1, R2, Arena, RBL, N1/2

Years Played – 2015-present

Positions/Roles – OF, 1B, scorekeeper R2, Manager in Arena League, Administrator in N1/2

Softball/Baseball/Other Sports Background - Division I college baseball player at Hofstra Univ in NY; have played softball for 40+ yrs.

Thoughts on softball here – Top rate facilities and people!

Key players, teammates, & others important to you – Many.

Other comments – Softball here is great! Where else do they drag fields every day and before each senior softball game?

Name/Age – Larry Dickerson, 79

Where Born? – Detroit, MI

Moved here from? – Orlando, FL

Job(s), Career – Mechanical Engineer – worked for Rockwell (aerospace); P&H (hydraulic cranes); Huffy (sporting goods); Amana (air conditioning). Started several businesses in Orlando – Grant Air; CDL Group; LD Industries;

Leagues & Divisions played in – R3, N3, RBL

Years Played – Since 2008

Positions/Roles – Presently 3B, 1B, SS

Softball/Baseball/Other Sports Background – HS football (kicker), baseball; Am Legion baseball; fast pitch softball till age 41; several championship teams over the years. Played every position except pitcher.

Thoughts on softball here – As older citizens we have matured in our thoughts and actions. We have discovered that winning isn't everything; if you lose, life goes on. We only feel down when we think we haven't given our best.

Key players, teammates, & others important to you – While there are players you are closer to than others, there is a special bond between all players. You don't care if one was the president of a large corporation or the janitor; a general or a private –

everyone is a 'good guy' and we really enjoy the camaraderie. Being around these guys, kidding each other, makes you feel young again.

Other comments – Even on my worst day – 0 for 4 with two errors – I give thanks. Life is good.

Author's Note: Larry was fortunate to play on three championship teams in 2013 – the Cowboys, R3; the Robins, RBL; and Hadley, N3.
In his fast pitch softball days, Larry was an outstanding base runner and fielder. He also had a 'different' specialty – getting hit by pitches. In the 1970s he was hit by a pitch on four consecutive at bats. Over one three year period he was hit by pitches 58 times! For anyone familiar with fast pitch softball, you know he had to have suffered a lot of bruises during that time. And he can still walk without a limp!
(I learned all of this from a newspaper article.)

Name/Age – Rick Duemler, 66

Where Born? – Wiesbaden FRG (Federal Republic of Germany) - Military father

Moved here from? – San Antonio, TX

Job(s), Career – Retired Lt. Col. U.S. Army – 24 yrs; Sr. Army Instructor for High School Jr. ROTC – 14 yrs.

Leagues & Divisions played in – R2, CFL, Arena

Years Played – 6

Positions/Roles - OF/LCF

Softball/Baseball/Other Sports Background - High school basketball and track

Thoughts on softball here – The most organized and best facilities of any league I've ever been in.

Key players, teammates, & others important to you – Dan List was the best manager; knew the players and the game.

Other comments - Players are all great guys and fun to play softball with.

Name/Age – Rick Egan, 70

Where Born? – Boston, MA

Moved here from? - California

Job(s), Career – President/CFO – Swift Engineering

Leagues & Divisions played in – R4, 68+, N4

Years Played – 2015 - Present

Positions/Roles – 1B, SF, P

Softball/Baseball/Other Sports Background – College basketball; fast pitch softball – pitcher Northeast; modified pitcher

Thoughts on softball here – Great group of guys; chance to feel young again.

Key players, teammates, & others important to you – Matt Spanier, John Cilento, Bob Tambellini, Terry Penrod, Dave Bigelow, Rick Sanford, Terry Fritts, Joe Grossman, Steve Lefebvre.

Name/Age – Tom Ellis, 68

Where Born? – Huntington, West Virginia

Moved here from? – Glendale, Arizona

Job(s), Career – Aluminum industry, industrial management

Leagues & Divisions played in – Rec. 5

Years Played – one year, 2019-2020

Positions/Roles – 2B, outfield

Softball/Baseball/Other Sports Background – Baseball/basketball in HS; golf/pickleball/billiards in this community; high school ref and umpire for 34 years – basketball, baseball, softball, volleyball, football; coached girls softball for a number of years.

Thoughts on softball here – It's been interesting. I'm used to using aluminum bats, not the composites. Most players seem to be very serious and dedicated.

Key players, teammates, & others important to you – It's my first year. Manager is Mike Welch. Teammates are dedicated.

Other comments – For new players, watch some games and learn about softball here before you do the evaluations. Hope to move up and play 68+ and Neighborhood leagues.

Name/Age – Ed Falconer, 60

Where Born? – Erie, PA

Moved here from? – Greenville, SC

Job(s), Career – Owner/Operator of Entertainment Co.; DJ; Sound & Lighting Engineer; Mtce. Director

Leagues & Divisions played in – N3, RBL

Years Played – 7 years

Positions/Roles – P, other positions as needed, manager

Softball/Baseball/Other Sports Background – HS wrestler; softball; black belt in Korean Dang Soo Do karate

Thoughts on softball here – The competitive spirit and love of the game among the players here is unmatched anywhere in the world, at any age.

Key players, teammates, & others important to you – Dan Kincaid, Ray Saberg, Jim Cantalupo, Mike Bernier, Wayne Grunewald

Other comments – It has been a true joy to play with and against some of the best softball players. We've still got it!

Name/Age – Dick Fetterman, 70

Where Born? – Berwick, PA

Moved here from? – Bloomsburg, PA - in 2010

Job(s), Career – 32 years with the U.S. Air Force and Air National Guard in the Communications field. Five years with the Pennsylvania Public Assistance Office.

Leagues & Divisions played in – R5, N5, R5K

Years Played - Third year in Rec 5K; 6 years in R5; and 6 years in N5.

Positions/Roles - OF

Softball/Baseball/Other Sports Background – Never played organized sports in HS or college; played intramurals in the military.

Thoughts on softball here – Softball provides great opportunities for exercise and camaraderie.

Key players, teammates, & others important to you – Got inspiration from guys like Dale Appleby in the R5 league who was still playing ball in his late 80's.

Other comments – I consider softball one of the best benefits of living in this community.

Name/Age – Maury Fjestad, 68

Where Born? – Fergus Falls, MN

Moved here from? – Apple Valley, MN

Job(s), Career – Computer System Software Support – 40 years.

Leagues & Divisions played in – N3, N4, CFL, R4, R3, R2

Years Played – Since 2013

Positions/Roles – P, SF, OF, scorekeeper

Softball/Baseball/Other Sports Background – Played in softball leagues every year since age 12. Player/manager for the same team for 40 years. Also played league volleyball for 35 years.

Thoughts on softball here – Very well run at all levels. The fields, with announcers and all, sold me on softball here in 2012.

Key players, teammates, & others important to you – Chad Smith, St. James neighborhood mgr (26 game win streak); Chuck Bowman, on his games played here; Pat Rice, on his comeback from surgeries; Wally Dias, on his player evaluations and playing attitude.

Other comments – I still recall a player prayer after one game, trusting that there would be softball in the afterlife, when we are done playing here.

Name/Age – Dave Foltz, 79

Where Born? – Ohio **Moved here from?** - Georgia

Job(s), Career – Aerospace/Defense Contractor

Leagues & Divisions played in – R1, R2, R3, RBL, 68+, Mid-Florida, Classics 70, Neighborhood, Florida Half Century

Years Played - 15

Positions/Roles – OF, Mid-Florida Commissioner

Softball/Baseball/Other Sports Background – League and travel softball, basketball

Thoughts on softball here – These fields are probably the best in the U.S. The player drafts each season in the Rec leagues maximizes parity. The mandatory evaluations aid this also. The umpire and administration tasks being handled by all volunteers is unique and works very well.

Key players, teammates, & others important to you – Dan List, Frenchie Le Tan, Dave Mamuscia, Dick Kanyan, Bob Fuhst, Jack Marx, Terry and Linda Yanny, Bill Johnson, Al Deibler, Duane Miller, Ev Arnold, Terry Cole, Joe Hathaway, and Joe Sanchez.

Other comments – Not sure who the oldest player is, but do know there are several 80+ players still 'swinging a bat.'

Name/Age – Ron Goldman, 69

Where Born? – Queens, NYC, NY

Moved here from? – Mineola, Long Island, NY

Job(s), Career – 30 yrs Auto Mechanic, 20 yrs Pharmaceuticals, Data Analyst

Leagues & Divisions played in – N3, R3, 68+, CFL, RBL

Years Played – 7

Positions/Roles – 3B, SS, SF, 2B, 1B

Softball/Baseball/Other Sports Background – Modified & Fast Pitch softball; Men's Senior Baseball League 1988-2007

Thoughts on softball here – When I walked onto the fields at Saddlebrook for the first time I was reminded of the scene from 'Field of Dreams' where Joe Jackson asks Kevin Costner, "Is this heaven?" His reply was, "No, this is Iowa." That could be replaced with 'No, this is The Villages.'

Key players, teammates, & others important to you – Dan List, player and manager in R2; played for many years with a fatal cancer diagnosis. He was the most respected man I ever had the pleasure of knowing.

Other comments – The fields and environment have created a sanctuary for me. Nothing negative enters my mind when I'm playing and 'BS-ing' with teammates.

Name/Age – Mark Goodwin, 70

Where Born? – Buffalo, NY

Moved here from? - Ukraine

Job(s), Career – Worked in Eastern Europe

Leagues & Divisions played in – R3, N3, 68+, CFL

Years Played - 8

Positions/Roles – SF, 1B, 2B, 3B, OF

Softball/Baseball/Other Sports Background –
Varsity football & wrestling letters in college at Rutgers

Thoughts on softball here – Great fun, keeps us
active, helps maintain a bit of 'competitive spirit.' But
most important – it is a game and we are blessed to be
able to play it at our age.

**Key players, teammates, & others important to
you** – Countless people!

Other comments – I always worked my butt off and
never had time to really make friends. So, here it is
great to walk into a softball complex and say hi, shout
out, tell jokes, or rib with the guys. Our bodies' may
realize where we are in life, but softball keeps our
minds in our teens.

Name/Age – Lindell Grigg, 72

Where Born? – Mulberry Grove, IL
Moved here from? – Gainesville, FL

Job(s), Career – Retired U.S. Air Force Officer and Pilot; Jr. AF ROTC Instructor

Leagues & Divisions played in – R2, R3, N2, N3, RBL, 68+

Years Played – Fall 2014 to present

Positions/Roles – Have played all positions, including P; umpire, manager, board member

Softball/Baseball/Other Sports Background – HS baseball; church and industrial league softball, both slow and fast pitch; sports at military bases – softball, soccer, volleyball, football; golf.

Thoughts on softball here - I came here with the intent of playing golf regularly. I had no idea about the softball. But since 2014, softball has become the main activity in both mine and my wife's life. I average playing 4 to 5 days per week. My wife, Joyce, has become a mainstay in the tower as scorer. She scores at least one and often two games a day in the Rec League. Softball has become a family affair.

As much as the physical aspect, softball is a social activity for us. We have met more really great folks through softball here and have created extremely close friendships with many of them, sharing good times both on and off the field. It's funny, but if we gather for a social activity, the guys will obviously sit to share war stories from the softball field, but many of the wives are just as involved in the discussion.

Amazingly, it doesn't matter what our previous lives/careers may have been, on the field we are just a bunch of old guys playing as hard to win a softball game as we did when we were 18; but so grateful to God that we have the health and mobility at our age to be out there playing. And after the game is over within minutes, all ill-feeling we may have had on the field are gone and we're sitting around, laughing about both our good plays and bad and have probably forgotten the final score, and often within 10 minutes probably even who we had just played. It's a great game and has become important to so many folks here.

Key players, teammates, & others important to you - I have met so many great folks, both men and women, I couldn't even begin to list them. I will just share, that I lost total vision in my right eye in 2005. I tried to play catch shortly after, and with the loss of depth perception, I had extreme difficulty just trying to catch a thrown ball. I thought, not only because of age, but also this loss, that I would certainly never be able to play organized softball again. Dave Williams is my neighbor. Dave stated he also had a vision issue and encouraged me to give it a try to the extent of even accompanying me to the evaluations. Had it not been for Dave, I probably would have never gotten involved in the sport here.

Other comments - My other main teammate and primary support is my wife, Joyce. When she's here and not in Indiana with the grandchildren, she never misses one of my games; often she will even hang around to support me when I have to umpire a game after I've played. She cheers me on when I play, and she picks me up after I've had a terrible game, trying to convince me that I am not the ONLY reason we lost the game, even though I know in my mind I was. A man couldn't ask for a more supportive, loving wife.

Name/Age - Wayne Grunewald, 69

Born - March Air Force Base, Riverside, California

Moved From - Cumming, Georgia

Jobs/Career - MBA/CPA and worked in Public Accounting for Arthur Andersen & Co for 3 years and as a Financial Controller at Plant, Division, and Corporate levels for Kimberly-Clark Corp and affiliates for 30 years.

Leagues and Years Played - N-3 (13 years), RBL (13 years), R-3 (12 years), CFL (4 years), 68+ (2 years)

Positions - 2B, SF, SS first 3 to 4 years and LCF, RCF last 9 to 10 years

Roles - Board of Directors (N-3 and RBL), Manager (N-3, RBL, CFL and 68+), Coordinator of Players (RBL)

Sports Background - 2 years of High School Varsity Baseball, Football and Wrestling and 1 year of Small College Baseball and Wrestling; managed men's and women's softball teams for about 10 years after college graduation.

Thoughts on Softball here - I never imagined that I would be playing softball in retirement. And many seasons I play in 4 leagues, so that is 5 game days and 1 practice day per week, so it really helps keep me in shape. It is great there are so many leagues to match each player's skill and competitive level, starting with the player evaluations. I have made so many friends playing softball in The Villages and probably know the names of at least 250 players. What a great way to spend a couple of hours on game days, year round. The softball organization and playing fields are first class. And the local newspaper coverage makes it fun, especially if you get your picture or name in the sports section.

Key Players - There are so many players who volunteer their time as Board members, Managers, Umpires, Scorekeepers and new player Evaluators to make the leagues work so well. I have never experienced this kind of volunteer commitment by so many willing people. It is hard to single out individuals, but I observed Wally Dias, Dan List, and Jack Nagle each give thousands of volunteer hours over many years to continuously improve softball here.

Other Comments - I doubt there is any other senior softball organization in the world that is run as well, from beginning to end. I have become so accustomed to what we have, that I often take for granted all that is involved.

Name/Age – Ron Guba, 70

Where Born? – Boston, MA

Moved here from? – Cape Cod, MA

Job(s), Career – Operations/Materials Manager – High Tech Manufacturing.

Leagues & Divisions played in – RBL, 68+, R3

Years Played – 2014 to present

Positions/Roles – 3B, 2B, SF, manager

Softball/Baseball/Other Sports Background – Played fast pitch softball and semi-pro baseball in my 20s; played in Cape Cod Old-Timers Softball League; coached youth soccer for 14 years, including Olympic Development Program.

Thoughts on softball here – Lots of opportunity for anyone to play – men, women, serious play, fun play, all skill levels. Great way to get exercise and meet people from all over the country and around our community. Very nice facilities and fields.

Key players, teammates, & others important to you – Many interesting and great people here. A few that had an influence on me:
Wayne Grunewald called and got me interested in RBL. He was great as my first manager. He gives a lot of himself to RBL and other community organizations.

139

Woody Wood – He managed the team the first time I subbed in RBL; very welcoming, friendly, and encouraging; a good demeanor, treats everyone well, a great teammate. Now, seven years later, as a manager myself, I often remember that.

Dean Hooker – Sets a great example. Fortunately, I've played for many teams he has managed. He's always pleasant and encouraging, drafts well, and wants everyone to have fun. His teams are always successful.

Other comments – One of the main reasons for me moving here was the extensive softball opportunities that are available.

Name/Age – Earl Hearst, 75

Where Born? – St. Louis, MO

Moved here from? - Maryland

Job(s), Career - Psychiatrist

Leagues & Divisions played in – R4, RBL, 68+, N4

Years Played - 9

Positions/Roles – 2B, 3B, SF

Softball/Baseball/Other Sports Background – Played baseball in Maryland Senior League. Medal winner – Senior Olympic table tennis

Thoughts on softball here – Great opportunity to find competitive play and social friends

Key players, teammates, & others important to you in – Greg Kuzbida, Vic Shearing, Bill Taylor

Name/Age – Paul R. Hein, 79

Where Born? – Queens, NY

Moved here from? – New Jersey

Job(s), Career – VP of Research and Development (Chemistry field); Professor of Chemistry–University of MD and Passaic Community College in NJ

Leagues & Divisions played in – R3, N3, 68+, Classic League, CFL, Travel Teams (70+, 75+)

Years Played – 2009 to present

Positions/Roles – SS, SF

Softball/Baseball/Other Sports Background -

Thoughts on softball here – It's the reason I moved to this community and I'm glad I did!

Key players, teammates, & others important to you – My mentor when I first moved here was William Hoffmeister.

Other comments – Pat Rice is one of the best pure hitters I know.

Name/Age – Michael Hendershot, 73

Where Born? – Newark, OH

Moved here from? – Columbus, OH

Job(s), Career – Medical Sales

Leagues & Divisions played in – R5, N5

Years Played - 7

Positions/Roles – OF, SF, Manager

Softball/Baseball/Other Sports Background – Golf, pickleball

Thoughts on softball here – It's a great way to meet people, while also being fun.

Key players, teammates, & others important to you – Bobby Davis, Wayne Meyer

Other comments – I thought I was going to play golf all the time. Now, however, I play softball more often.

Name/Age –Ed Hewitt, 73

Where Born? – Gary, IN

Moved here from? – Ogden Dunes, IN

Job(s), Career – VP of a construction company

Leagues & Divisions played in – R3, R4, N3, N4,
68+, RBL   **Years Played** - 5

Positions/Roles – 3B, SS, 2B, OF, scorer, umpire

Softball/Baseball/Other Sports Background –
Learned to play pickleball when we were snowbirds 8
years ago and joined USPA. Have played in tourneys in
IL, MI, and IN. Ran my first 5K when we moved here
full time, at age 70, during the Disney marathon week.
Thoughts on softball here – The 1st softball field I
saw here was the new Soaring Eagle complex. It was
beautiful. I thought I was 10 years old again and I was
hooked. They announce your name when you come to
the plate. They also keep batting averages and put
results in the newspaper!
**Key players, teammates, & others important to
you** – I've met players who played NCAA DI in college
and I played with a guy 5 years ago who was 82 and
cold still run and hit; and he took less medication than I
did!
Other comments – Manager Billy Taylor knew every
player, their abilities, and put them together as a team.
The volunteers make this all possible. It gives us old
guys the thoughts of being semi-competitive and young
once again.

Name/Age – Mark Hildebrand, 70

Where Born? – Cincinnati, OH
Moved here from? – Cincinnati, OH
Job(s), Career – Police Officer

Leagues & Divisions played in – R3, R2, R1, N3, CFL, Arena, Travel Teams, Classics, Veterans Tourney
Years Played – 2007 - present

Positions/Roles – Middle IF; Manager Vets Teams
Softball/Baseball/Other Sports Background – Golf and pickleball

Thoughts on softball here – For me, it is more about the relationships with my teammates than winning or losing. Playing softball makes me feel younger than I am! I started in Div 3 and gradually moved up to Div 1; this has allowed me to expand my group of contacts and foster a wide range of lasting friendships. I am most proud to have received the Joel Beason MVP award in CFL for 2011.

Key players, teammates, & others important to you – Billy Warble, Ed Haith, Don Giesler, and Rod Severson are the most recent managers who have influenced me in such a positive way. They exhibit leadership, dedication, and humor. My twilight years would not be the same without their friendship and support.

Other comments – No place in this great country could I experience the lifestyle and camaraderie which takes place here. I am so fortunate to have found it.

Name/Age – Doug Hinkel, 78

Where Born? – Washington, D.C.

Moved here from? – Virginia Beach, VA

Job(s), Career – Peace Corps-Ecuador teaching English and sports; Loan Officer, Computer Analyst, Programmer, and Manager for a large Federal Credit Union; Computer Consultant.

Leagues & Divisions played in – R3, R4, R5, N3, N4, RBL, 68+, Classic 70s

Years Played – 11 in The Villages; 35+ in Virginia Beach, northern VA, and Bradenton, FL

Positions/Roles – Mostly P; some C, 1B, RF

Softball/Baseball/Other Sports Background – LL and HS baseball; HS basketball and track; college track and field at William & Mary (sprints, relays, hurdles, long jump, javelin); coached youth soccer, track/field, football, basketball, baseball; play water volleyball, pickleball, and tennis here; discus, shot put, javelin, and sprints in Senior Games in VA and FL.

Thoughts on softball here – Being evaluated on skill level, not just age, makes for great competition and enjoyment. The variety of leagues and the outstanding fields keeps the experience fresh and alive for both newer and veteran players.

Key players, teammates, & others important to you – Praise for all the volunteers-Boards, managers, umpires, statisticians, scorers, online webmasters, etc. Too many special teammates and managers to list them all. Here is a remembered event – during 2009 evaluations me and one other player were hitting very long balls and some of mine were further. Nowadays, he is playing in the higher leagues still 'smacking the ball a mile' while I am in the lower leagues barely able to hit a long ball or run the bases!

Other comments – Play for fun and the association with comrades. As you age or have physical/injury problems, you will have good and not so great seasons. Just keep going until it's time to retire from playing, but remember that you can still continue as a manager, umpire, etc.

Name/Age – Paul Hoecker, 70

Where Born? – Chicago, IL

Moved here from? – Atlanta, GA

Job(s), Career – SE Regional V-P for AIG, Inc.

Leagues & Divisions played in – 68+, N3

Years Played – Since the fall of 2014

Positions/Roles – Have played every position except pitcher

Softball/Baseball/Other Sports Background - Played 16" softball in Chicago in the 1970s.

Thoughts on softball here – Love it! When we first came to visit in 2014 and saw softball being played at Buffalo Glen, I told my wife, "We're moving here."

Key players, teammates, & others important to you – Too numerous to mention. In Neighborhood leagues, I have played for Glenbrook, Virginia Trace, Tamarind Grove, Lake Deaton, and Deaton/Hills.

Other comments – I couldn't wait to turn 68 and join the 68+ league! I've played with the Cobras, Hellcats, Hornets, and the Barracudas.

Name/Age – Dean A. Hooker, 70

Where Born? – Bluefields, Nicaragua

Moved here from? – Cairo, Egypt

Job(s), Career – Civil Engineer, Business Degree, IT

Leagues & Divisions played in – R3, N3, 68+, CFL, RBL

Years Played – Since 2013

Positions/Roles – All positions except pitcher

Softball/Baseball/Other Sports Background - Little League baseball, soccer, volleyball, bowling, and fishing

Thoughts on softball here – Best organized leagues I have played in. Facilities are outstanding.

Key players, teammates, & others important to you – Ron Goldman, who I call my 'sensei' (Asian, meaning teacher). He is a great guy who cares and shares his knowledge of the game with any player who asks. He has taught me all that I know about becoming a good softball player.

Name/Age – Bob Hrabak, 70

Where Born? – Chicago, IL

Moved here from? – Tampa, FL

Job(s), Career – Banking, retired

Leagues & Divisions played in – R4, N4, 68+, Veterans Tourney

Years Played – 11 yrs.

Positions/Roles – Manager in Neighborhood and Rec; did Veterans Tournament for 10 yrs; also D4 state tournament; D4 umpire. Played every position at one time or another over the years.

Softball/Baseball/Other Sports Background – Managed Little League, girls' softball, Rec football & basketball; played 5 yrs men's softball in Tampa.

Thoughts on softball here – I've played lots of age 40+ softball and this community has the best complexes anywhere.

Key players, teammates, & others important to you – Since I started playing here in 2009, the D4 players are my family. They take care of each other and with prayers as needed. We're friends forever.

Other comments – Softball in all ways is "the best way of life!"

Name/Age – Paul Isenberg, 64

Where Born? – Pittsburgh, PA

Moved here from? – S. Florida, near Ft. Lauderdale

Job(s), Career – 38 years with FedEx, mostly in management, in PA, WV, VA, and south FL.

Leagues & Divisions played in – R3, R2, Arena, CFL, RBL, N3, N1/2

Years Played – 5+ years; did not play before that.

Positions/Roles – All but P, SS; mostly OF; manager

Softball/Baseball/Other Sports Background – Didn't really play anything, except some golf.

Thoughts on softball here – Softball here is great; a good chance to socialize and meet people while still playing a game!

Key players, teammates, & others important to you – I've met so many people from D1 to D5. They have all been important.

Other comments – I served on the D3 Board and will soon find out if I will be on the D2 Board. I managed in RBL and the Arena League (1st place!) I've been involved in player drafts in RBL, Arena, D3, D2, and CFL; as well as new player evaluations for over a year.

Name/Age – Darren Ivey, 54

Where Born? – Warner Robins, GA

Moved here from? – Leesburg, FL

Job(s), Career – U.S. Army; Service Technician for Sprint Telephone

Leagues & Divisions played in – N3, RBL, R3

Years Played - 3

Positions/Roles – 3B, SF, 2B, OF, manager

Softball/Baseball/Other Sports Background – Played softball as a teenager; also while in the Army; and two years after leaving the military.

Thoughts on softball here – I love the game. I play four days a week. The leagues seem to have 'even' teams with the draft and all.

Key players, teammates, & others important to you – So many! I have a very personal friendship with Dean Hooker, who took me under his wing to make me a better player. I'm also close with Herb Lauer and Ray Walters.

Other comments – Softball is a big part of my life and also my wife's. She is an official assistant manager on my R3 team. Tina helps with many things – keeping the scorebook, sending out emails, and much more.

Name/Age – Ernie Joyal, 71

Where Born? – Putnam, CT

Moved here from? – Springfield, VA

Job(s), Career – Program Manager, Naval Undersea Warfare Center

Leagues & Divisions played in – R4, N4, 68+, RBL

Years Played – 2006 - present

Positions/Roles – OF, Manager

Softball/Baseball/Other Sports Background - HS basketball and football

Thoughts on softball here - It's 'Senior Softball Heaven'

Key players, teammates, & others important to you – Matt Spanier, who runs the 68+ league, manages teams, and sits on the Board of Rec. 4

Other comments – I am privileged to play year round in such a well managed softball program with fantastic facilities – with so many men of honor.

Name/Age – Dick Kanyan, 76

Where Born? – Indiana, PA

Moved here from? – Pomfret, MD

Job(s), Career – Securities & Exchange Commission in D.C. Hired as a Clerk at age 17 and retired 37 ½ yrs later as Operations Officer.

Leagues & Divisions played in – R1, R2, Arena, Classic 70s, N 1/2, Mid-Florida 55+, 60+, Florida Half Century (FHC). Numerous titles over the years.

Years Played - 20

Positions/Roles – All 11 positions at one time or another; Mgr., Co-Mgr., Ump, Scorekeeper. In charge of Operations for Florida Half Century and Nat'l teams.

Softball/Baseball/Other Sports Background – Fast pitch in D.C. 1963-67; slow pitch in MD till 2000. Two world champion teams, 1999, 2010. Numerous nat'l titles over the years, as well as FHC titles. FHC Hall of Fame; Rec. 1 Field of Honor. Many medals in local, state, and nat'l Senior Games – softball, table tennis, volleyball, shuffleboard, basketball, and badminton.

Thoughts on softball here – A wonderful place to play softball. Talented, well-mannered players at all levels. We have fun. Good camaraderie. Strong sense of community – outings, golf, dinner, wives do things together, etc.

One of my most exciting and enjoyable seasons was playing in Rec 2 for the Orioles in 2017. I was drafted to play 1st base, but circumstances came about that I volunteered to pitch. Ended up with a 15-3 record. I had the good fortune to have an outstanding offensive and defensive team behind me. The Orioles won the regular season championship.

Key players, teammates, & others important to you – Jack Marx – one of the most winning mgrs for Travel Teams. Keen sense of identifying talent. Frenchie Le Tan – Probably done more to promote softball than anyone; has a passion and love for the game; extremely competitive. Dave Mamuscia – Very dedicated in everything he is involved with, especially softball; always willing to help out.

Others include: Ev Arnold, Bob Buchanan, Sal Colloca, Paul Duda, Gregg Foster, Doug Gerkin, Ron Gustaitis, Roy Hern, Ralph Hollis, Lenny Iancale, Al Mahar, Tom McGann, Gary Nicolay, John Rebardo, Roger Scott, Dave Sellars, Rod Severson, Bud Shelley, Tom Simmons, Mike Stein, John Tehonica, Carl McWilliams, Peter Velez, John Wick; many, many others.

Other comments – Softball is a team sport – every player is important, as are managers and coaches. My wife, Pat, is supportive, understanding and has been a large part of my success. We've had 55 wonderful years of marriage.

Name/Age – George Kennedy, 76

Where Born? – Bronx, NY

Moved here from? – New City/West Nyack, NY

Job(s), Career – Detective NYPD; Senior Investigator NYS Comm. of Invest; and Vernon Corp.

Leagues & Divisions played in – N1, N2, N3, Rec. 1 Rec. 2, CFL, RBL

Years Played -18

Positions/Roles – Infield, Umpire

Softball/Baseball/Other Sports Background – All seasonal sports, softball in Bar Leagues and NYPD League, coached Little League and Babe Ruth

Thoughts on softball here –Great fields; well organized at all levels; honored to have the 2019 Veterans Tournament named after my son, Major Thomas E. Kennedy – KIA in 2012.

Key players, teammates, & others important to you – Playing with guys from all over this great country of ours; too many to list.

Other comments – After not playing for 30 years, my mind was saying 'do this' and my body was saying 'what are you doing?' Now I'm just trying to keep the "old man out." I'm still loving it and thanking God I'm still able to do it.

Name/Age – Gil Kettelhut, 66

Where Born? – Kansas City, Missouri

Moved here from? – Omaha, Nebraska

Job(s), Career – High School Principal and Superintendent of Schools

Leagues & Divisions played in – Neighborhood 3, Rec 3, RBL

Years Played - 7

Positions/Roles – Mostly outfield, current Rec 3 commissioner and board member

Softball/Baseball/Other Sports Background – Baseball pitcher in high school and also in leagues after college; high school tennis coach for 15 years

Thoughts on softball here – As Charles Dickens wrote in the first part of A Tale of Two Cities, "It was the best of times......."

Key players, teammates, & others important to you – Ray Walters was a great mentor to me in taking on the Commissioner's role.

Other comments – Softball in The Villages has been a great run for me in terms of being with wonderful individuals both on and off the fields.

Name/Age – Fred King, 64

Where Born? – Duluth, MN

Moved here from? – Franklin, WI (Milwaukee area)

Job(s), Career – Retired as Alternate Channel Director of Finance, SE Region for ATT

Leagues & Divisions played in – N2, N3, Rec3, RBL

Years Played – 11-12 years

Positions/Roles – Pitcher, OF, Rec. 3 Board

Softball/Baseball/Other Sports Background - High school and JC basketball; never played baseball or softball until moving to The Villages.

Thoughts on softball here –For all skill levels and senior ages, this is a tremendous operation. Fields and facilities are great – out-of-towners here for tourneys comment on that. The volunteers running the leagues are great, as is the player camaraderie.

Key players, teammates, & others important to you – Too many to name; all players and managers have been great. Chuck Bowler puts in many hours handling D3 computer data bases and technical issues with our statistical records.

Other comments – The fact that we're a bunch of old retired guys playing this game at this level and with these facilities says it all.

Name/Age – Jack Kleffman, 78

Where Born? – Chicago, IL

Moved here from? – Palos Heights, IL

Job(s), Career - Mailman

Leagues & Divisions played in – R2, R3, R4, N2, N3, N4, 68+, 70+

Years Played - 17

Positions/Roles – SS, SF, P

Softball/Baseball/Other Sports Background – None

Thoughts on softball here – Great way to grow old!

Key players, teammates, & others important to you – Jack Meagher, Matt Spanier, Fran Nencetti

Other comments – I have worked evaluations for 15 years.

Name/Age – Ed Krisha, 74

Where Born? – Cleveland, OH

Moved here from? – Houston, TX

Job(s), Career – Information Systems Development Manager

Leagues & Divisions played in – R1, R2, R3, N1/2, N3, CFL, Classics, FL Half Century Travel Team (Florida State Champs in 2018)

Years Played – 2008 – 2018

Positions/Roles – All IF positions, P; CFL Board; Manager.

Softball/Baseball/Other Sports Background – All HS sports; AAU basketball 10 yrs; Cleveland City Softball Leagues; Navy teams 1964-68.

Thoughts on softball here – Well thought out rules, structure, and competition for all levels. Wonderfully social group – after 2 or 3 seasons you suddenly have 300 new friends!

Key players, teammates, & others important to you – Jack Marx – wonderful guy; taught me how to live a better life; and how to manage and play for fun and enjoyment. Al Krause – Cleveland native, taught me how to pitch effectively – to pitch curve balls, screw balls, and knuckleballs; a fantastic coach and mentor.

Name/Age – Dana Lambillotte, 72

Where Born? – Barberton, OH

Moved here from? – Sandusky, OH

Job(s), Career - Management

Leagues & Divisions played in – R2, R3, 68+, RBL, CFL   **Years Played** – January 2015 to present

Positions/Roles – All positions except pitcher; also serve as umpire and manager.

Softball/Baseball/Other Sports Background – Stopped playing softball in 1978 until arriving here. Did a few weekend athletic activities.

Thoughts on softball here – Thankful to be physically and financially able to play softball again.

Key players, teammates, & others important to you – Hundreds! Some playing with artificial knees and hips and playing well; others fighting cancer. The desire to play competitively is still there. For them the fire has not gone out. And what a joy to be playing while your kids, grandkids, and even great grandkids are in the stands watching.

Other comments – Perhaps our legacy is to show the next generation that there is life after work. You play a game as a kid, work 30-40 years, and then get to play again.

Name/Age – Herb Lauer, 58

Where Born? – Cheverly, MD

Moved here from? – Lorton, VA

Job(s), Career – Produce Manager for Safeway

Leagues & Divisions played in – Neighborhood 3, Rec 3, RBL, CFL

Years Played – Since 2017

Positions/Roles – 1B, 2B, 3B, outfield/umpire

Softball/Baseball/Other Sports Background – Played baseball till age 14. Coached and umpired for women's softball. Began playing men's softball, but was inactive for 20 years until moving here.

Thoughts on softball here – I've been blessed to be able to get back playing. What a great thrill!

Key players, teammates, & others important to you – Tom Bortle and Doug St. Andrews took me under their wings early on. Ron Pask took a chance and drafted me on his team.

Other comments – I've met some wonderful people playing softball. Great memories, priceless, will never forget these times and people. And I tell all players to stretch, stretch, and stretch some more before games.

Name/Age – Billy Layton, 74

Where Born? – Concord, NC

Moved here from? – Charlotte, NC

Job(s), Career – Radar man on destroyers in the Navy, 1964-70; graduated UNC-Charlotte, '73; CPA and held various accounting/finance positions until 2000

Leagues & Divisions and years – Rec leagues – started at Knudson in 2001 and played 3 seasons; moved to B, later re-named Rec 2, in 2002 and played 40 seasons; moved to Rec 3 in 2016; have served as ump, mgr., Bd member, scorekeeper in leagues.
N leagues – played for Belle Aire starting 2002; managed N1/2 and 466 North team; moved to Belle Aire N3 team in 2016; also umpired.
Arena – Managed and umpired for about 10 years.

Positions Played - Every position at one time or another; I only pitched once, in R2, when our regular pitcher did not show up. Nowadays, I play mostly 1B, C, 2B, and RF.

Softball/Baseball/Other Sports Background - None, except pickup games in the Navy.

Thoughts on softball here – Fun to re-live childhood experiences, but it is so much more. First class facilities. We come from so many backgrounds and areas of the country, but softball brings us together to enjoy each other's company in the game we love.

Key players, teammates, & others important to you – So many, but includes Charlie Monton, Joe Sanchez, Al Shirmer, John Rebardo, Avis Vaught, Lew Jones, Terry Cole, Bob Baker, Don Barnes, Bill DiCarlo, Dan List, Gary Grodzicki, and Beaver Burch.

Other comments – As a small child, my granddaughter Courtney Layton got to see me play softball here. She is now a rising senior at East Carolina University and plays on the softball team there. I proudly wear her #21 on my softball jersey each season. It doesn't get any better than that!

Name/Age – Frenchie Le Tan, 87

Where Born? – Philadelphia, PA

Moved here from? – Pasadena, MD

Job(s), Career – Managed a sporting goods store for Brooks Robinson of the Baltimore Orioles; later was a partner with pro baseball's John Orsino and pro basketball's Gene Shue in similar ventures. Owned Pro-Line Enterprise, a sporting goods company. Was also in Wine & Liquor sales in Baltimore.

Leagues & Divisions played in – R1, R2, Classics, Half Century Travel Teams

Years Played – Almost 20 years locally

Positions/Roles – SS, 1B, Classics League Manager and Commissioner, Half Century Manager

Softball/Baseball/Other Sports Background – HS football, baseball, basketball; some lacrosse. Offered Div I basketball scholarship, but turned it down to sign to play professional baseball instead. Played two years of minor league baseball. Played semi-pro football as a QB and punter. Tried out as punter for the Baltimore Colts, but was cut. Served as a pro baseball scout for Baltimore and Milwaukee. Played Eastern Seaboard League fast pitch softball for almost 40 years. In high school, I played baseball against future major leaguer Al Kaline (Detroit Tigers); and other baseball against Barry Shetrone, who later played for the Baltimore Orioles and Washington Senators.

Thoughts on softball here – This is the very best program in the country. It is run by fine people. Everyone can play here no matter what their skill level because of the five divisions.

Key players, teammates, & others important to you – Frankie Murth, Bob Furst, Ev Arnold, Dewey McVicker, Don Duell, and Digger Lines, who pitched in the majors for the Senators. Furst, Arnold, McVicker, and Duell are all in national softball Halls of Fame.

Other comments – I was fortunate to play for great sponsors like Munn's in the Classics League and Frankie Brin Financial in the Half Century League. I have also put on a golf tournament sponsored by Frankie Brin's at Orange Blossom for the past 15 years. We have 72 golfers in the tournament each year.

Name/Age – Bob Loeffler, 79

Where Born? – Sandusky, OH

Moved here from? – Bedford, OH

Job(s), Career – Math teacher at Bedford HS for 35 years; Baseball coach 32 years.

Leagues & Divisions played in – R3, N3

Years Played - 14

Positions/Roles – SS, C, Manager

Softball/Baseball/Other Sports Background – Played baseball in high school and at Kent State; played Class A baseball in Cleveland from 1962-1966.

Thoughts on softball here – Everything is really great!

Key players, teammates, & others important to you – Wally Dias, Jim Holloway, Gil Kettlehut, John Fink, Chuck Bowler

Other comments -
I wish I was still 66 like I was when I first got here!

Name/Age – Steve Long, 72

Where Born? – Hanover, PA

Moved here from? – Pasadena, MD

Job(s), Career – Data Processing Software

Leagues & Divisions played in – R1, Classic 70s, Arena, Frankie Brin 70s

Years Played – 16 yrs in The Villages

Positions/Roles - IF

Softball/Baseball/Other Sports Background – Coached fast pitch for 30 yrs; umpired fast pitch, slow pitch, and baseball

Thoughts on softball here – Best senior softball in Florida.

Key players, teammates, & others important to you – Just about everyone; too many to mention.

Other comments – Enjoy the camaraderie.

Name/Age – Carlos Lopez, 76

Where Born? – Panama Canal Zone

Moved here from? – Simi Valley, CA

Job(s), Career – Manufacturing/Mechanical Engineer

Leagues & Divisions played in – Div. 3, CFL

Years Played – Since 2004

Positions/Roles – SS, P

Softball/Baseball/Other Sports Background - Played soccer when young

Thoughts on softball here - It's a great activity

Key players, teammates, & others important to you – Way too many to name all of them, but some are: Ron Nikstad, Tom DiSalvo, Charlie Manning, Jeff Bekasi, Jim Domingos, Pat Rice, Ron Lottes, and Fred Storcks

Other comments – Have warm memories of some players who are no longer with us. I especially miss Mark Froehle and Dan List.

Name/Age – Ron Lottes, 74

Where Born? – Huntingburg, IN

Moved here from? – Des Moines, IA

Job(s), Career – Exec V-P Wells Fargo Financial and COO of its US Consumer Lending Operations

Leagues & Divisions played in – R3, N3

Years Played – Since 2002

Positions/Roles – 1B, C, SF, P, manager, R3 Board, Softball Advisory Board

Softball/Baseball/Other Sports Background - HS basketball, football, baseball

Thoughts on softball here – Softball in The Villages is an environment for creating friends for the rest of our lives. The camaraderie that develops between the players is amazing.

Key players, teammates, & others important to you – Tom McGann, Tom Burish, Pete McCaffrey, Ed Chirumbolo, Lew Jones, Ron Nikstad, Ed Moriarity

Other comments – Playing softball is an activity that most of us thought was in our past, but we were able to move to The Villages and return to our 'yesteryears.' R3 has been a place where great friendships developed and will last the rest of our lives.

Name/Age – Dave Mamuscia, 77

Where Born? – Auburn, NY
Moved here from? – Brighton, MI

Job(s), Career – Health Insurance Actuary
Leagues & Divisions played in – D1 (2006-2015), D2 (2015), tournament teams (2006-2020), Classics
Years Played – 2006-2020
Positions/Roles – P, OF, 1B, C, Sec./Treas.-Classics
Softball/Baseball/Other Sports Background – Softball, volleyball, and pickup basketball in MI

Thoughts on softball here – It's great! Perhaps its greatest strength is the process for selecting teams to ensure competitive balance. And when the teams are re-drafted 3 times/yr, you meet a wide variety of other players. The system of Divisions allows players to compete with others of similar abilities and skills, so that everyone can enjoy the game and not feel out of place.
Key players, teammates, & others important to you – Too numerous to mention all; but a core group of Dick Kanyan, Dave Sellars, Rod Severson, Roger Scott, and Jack Marx. Our teams were among the best in the nation, winning a number of national tourneys and dozens in Florida Half Century.
Other comments – I was a pretty ordinary player when younger (and still am). I never imagined being able to play this much softball through my mid-70s with players who perform at such a high level. It's been a dream come true.

Name/Age – Bob Marano, 82

Where Born? – White Plains, NY

Moved here from? – White Plains, NY

Job(s), Career – General Manager - Wallauer Paint and Decorating Center

Leagues & Divisions played in – R1, R2, R3, R4, R5, Classic 70s, Mid-Florida, CFL, 68+, Half Century

Years Played - 17

Positions/Roles – Every position on the field

Softball/Baseball/Other Sports Background - Pickleball, golf

Thoughts on softball here – Before coming to The Villages, I heard they had the best senior softball in the country. I've not been disappointed yet.

Key players, teammates, & others important to you – Dick Lyons, Gino Dell, Dave Foltz, Ev Arnold, Doug Gerkin, Milt Hershey and many more.

Other comments – I've been playing senior softball since I was 55 years old. I've participated in many national tournaments all over the U.S. and Canada. I've played for Pompano Beach Bums, Old South, New Jersey Jaguars, and Frankie Brin.

Name/Age – Jack Marx, 76

Where Born? – Streator, IL

Moved here from? – St. Louis, MO

Job(s), Career – Electrical Engineer, graduate of Univ of Illinois at Champaign-Urbana

Leagues & Divisions played in – I've played in all Rec Divisions 1-5, as well as Travel Teams w/Florida Half Century. When I first started playing here, we had only two teams - before the Rec Leagues were formed. Now we have 5 Divisions with many teams in each Division.

Years Played - 19

Positions/Roles – OF, Manager

Softball/Baseball/Other Sports Background - Played baseball my whole life; softball in college.

Thoughts on softball here - I believe that the early success of our teams in the Florida Half Century travel league influenced a lot of players from other areas of Florida to move here to play softball.

Key players, teammates, & others important to you – Dick Kanyan, Ken Atkinson, Scott Marshall, Terry Yanny, Ed Kordus, Al Mahar, Bill Cini

Other comments – I really love the game of softball!

Name/Age – Pete McCaffrey, 62

Where Born? – Denver, CO

Moved here from? – Las Vegas, NV

Job(s), Career – Colonel U.S. Air Force; Fighter Pilot-33 Year career; Retired pilot for United Air Lines.

Leagues & Divisions played in – R2, R3, N1/2, N3, RBL

Years Played – 2012 to present

Positions/Roles – SS, SF, 3B, OF

Softball/Baseball/Other Sports Background - Basketball, football, baseball – 4-yr starter for the U.S. Air Force Academy.

Thoughts on softball here – Softball here is not only a fun and wonderful way to get exercise, but also one of the best ways to make new friends and share in the lives of others.

Key players, teammates, & others important to you – Too many to mention.

Other comments – As a U.S. Air Force pilot, flew as a member of the Thunderbirds Air Demonstration Squadron from 1992-1995, as one of the solo pilots.

Name/Age – Thomas McGann, 76

Where Born? - Connecticut

Moved here from? - Connecticut

Job(s), Career – Southern New England Telephone Repairman – 2nd level management. Wrote payroll system, all field procedures for mechanized payroll.

Leagues & Divisions played in – N1/2, R2, R3, CFL Arena, Classics League, Travel Teams, Frankie Brin 74s, out-of-state tourneys, military/veteran tourneys.

Years Played – 2006-present

Positions/Roles – SF, SS, 2B, CFL Board, President of Classics League, numerous championships and rings. Managed Div 2 and 3, winning championships in each. Umpire in all leagues.

Softball/Baseball/Other Sports Background – Little League manager 30 years; softball batting instructor to present; Cape Cod Travel Team 2012-15.

Thoughts on softball here – Without a doubt, the reason I'm alive today. The ultimate fun in The Villages. Wonderful friendships. Love playing and teaching.

Key players, teammates, & others important to you – Pat Rice, best hitting mechanics; Ed Moriarity, great team player and top SS; Tom Gilewski, pitcher extraordinaire; Mark Hildebrand and Pat Rice, long ball hitters; Dan List, manager; Wally Dias, friend, pitcher and organizer R3.

Other comments – Memories: championships and titles at all levels; hitting OTF HR in R3; about 16 OTF homers all together; hitting .746 to win an unofficial batting title; but the best part is the friendships. Regarding the veteran tournaments, a top memory is meeting a WWII marine who carried the flag up Iwo Jima (Leo Champagne). I was shaking like a leaf when I met him.

Name/Age – Matthew Merrill, 64

Where Born? – River Rouge, MI

Moved here from? – Commerce Twp., MI

Job(s), Career – Facility Engineer - Chrysler

Leagues & Divisions played in – R5, N5

Years Played - 1

Positions/Roles – IF, OF

Softball/Baseball/Other Sports Background – Played all sports when young. Had not played softball in 40 years.

Thoughts on softball here – The fields are in great shape. The other players are helpful and friendly, which makes it a fun experience. A great place to play softball!

Key players, teammates, & others important to you – Everyone has been helpful. The Hoosiers in R5 and Fenney in N5 are my first teams.

Other comments – The volunteers keep things going – the umpires, field crews, scorekeepers, and others behind the scenes that are unknown to the new players like me.

Name/Age – Donny Meyer, 59

Where Born? – Flushing, NY

Moved here from? - NY

Job(s), Career – Retired NYPD

Leagues & Divisions played in – R1, Travel Teams

Years Played - 8

Positions/Roles – SS, SF, P

Softball/Baseball/Other Sports Background – Three different softball Halls of Fame (HOF) – NY Police Softball HOF; National Police Softball HOF; USSSA HOF.

Thoughts on softball here – Very competitive; great fields. I also run a travel team called Backspin Seating. We play in the Florida Half Century League. We're currently #9 in the state.

Key players, teammates, & others important to you – Henry Culley, Dave Norval, Steve Wilson – have played with or against them over the last 25 yrs.

Other comments – Have made numerous friends.

Name/Age – Wayne Meyer, 76

Where Born? – Philadelphia, PA

Moved here from? – Lafayette, IN

Job(s), Career – Management Consultant, business owner

Leagues & Divisions played in – Rec 3 – 35 seasons; Rec 4 – 2 seasons; Rec 5 – 14 seasons; N3

Years Played – 17 years

Positions/Roles – 2B, OF, P (one inning); Manager, Board, Commissioner

Softball/Baseball/Other Sports Background - Baseball in high school and in college at Pennsylvania Military College.

Thoughts on softball here - Great fields; well cared for.

Key players, teammates, & others important to you – Every player has their own story and background.

Name/Age – Paul "Tony" Mitchell, 73

Where Born? – Boston, MA

Moved here from? – Groton, CT

Job(s), Career – 25 yrs police officer in S. Kingstown, Rhode Island

Leagues & Divisions played in – R3, R2, R4, N2, RBL; several years on the Navy teams D3 and D4 for the Veterans Tourneys; one season on a travel team.

Years Played – 2002 to present

Positions/Roles - OF

Softball/Baseball/Other Sports Background – No baseball as a youngster; archery, bowling, golf; first softball was when we moved to The Villages.

Thoughts on softball here – The guys are great to play ball with; most of the time the teams are evenly matched; very much fun.

Key players, teammates, & others important to you – Danny List, Frank Ellard, Mike Garvin; all of the different people I play with.

Other comments – Have played in the RBL League since it started with a lot of fun guys.

Name/Age – Charlie Monton, 86

Where Born? – Custer, MI

Moved here from? – Ludington, MI

Job(s), Career – Farmed in lower MI from boyhood until 1985. A variety of farm animals in the early years and then dairy farming later on with Holstein cattle.

Leagues & Divisions played in – R3, R4, R5K, N3, N4, N5 and the Employee League.

Years Played – 1997-2009

Positions/Roles – C, P, 2B, OF, ump, Boards, and Commissioner at Knudson; field mtce at all fields.

Softball/Baseball/Other Sports Background - No sports growing up – all work on the farm.

Thoughts on softball here– It's been great to be involved with it.

Key players, teammates, & others important to you – Uda Hermans helped oversee and coordinate things at Knudson early on; Don Fraley was the first scorekeeper; Managers – Jerry May, Doug Barri; my supervisors for mtce. – John Rohan, Jack Ware, and Danny Jacobs.

Other comments – People have been good to me. I have really enjoyed being involved with the softball programs here.

Name/Age – Ed Moriarity, 71

Where Born? – LaSalle, IL
Moved here from? – Momence, IL

Job(s), Career – Junior High Teacher – Math, Phys Ed; Coach – baseball, track, basketball

Leagues & Divisions played in – R3, N1/2, N3, Mid-Florida, CFL, Florida Half Century travel team
Years Played – 2005-present
Positions/Roles – All positions, but mostly SS; CFL manager

Softball/Baseball/Other Sports Background – Softball and baseball till age 27, then all softball until age 52; quit for five years until moving to The Villages. Rugby and track in college; golf

Thoughts on softball here – Much different than what I had been told; much better. There are some very good players here. You can play at whatever level you want – serious competition or more relaxed leagues.
Key players, teammates, & others important to you – Bobby Winder, Gary Carr, Wally Dias, Jack Nesci, Tom McGann, Carlos Lopez, Pat Rice, Mariano Ramos to name a few.
Other comments – Some of the best opportunities anywhere; facilities are great; the number of people and teams is unmatched; softball here gives you everything you could ask for – good fun, good competition, and good friends.

Name/Age – Jack Nagle, almost an octogenarian

Where Born? – Long Island, NY

Moved here from? – Stockton, CA

Job(s), Career – High school English teacher for four years in NY and CA; then university professor and Dean of Education for almost 40 years at six universities in PA, OR, IL, VA, NC, and CA.

Leagues & Divisions played in – R3, N3, CFL, RBL

Years Played – Every season since fall of 2008; 36 consecutive seasons (3 per year).

Positions/Roles – Pitched initially, then mostly OF, and more recently IF, primarily at SF. Manager for Sunset Pointe in N3; Chief umpire N3; Board member N3; currently RBL Commissioner; umpire in all leagues

Softball/Baseball/Other Sports Background – Little League and Jr high baseball; then turned to band, orchestra, and chorus. Worked as waiter in dining hall for four years at Hamilton College, then on to grad school, teaching, and higher education. No softball for 50 years till moving here in 2008; have since played in over 1500 games of senior softball.

Thoughts on softball here – It's pretty special – well organized; competitive; well maintained fields; new balls each game; scorekeepers/scoreboards; great camaraderie; opportunities to play with many different folks; strong commitments to teams, rules, schedules, and safety of others. Players have unquestioned concern for the welfare of others.

Key players, teammates, & others important to you – Too many to identify individually. But that's the beauty of softball here. Everyone contributes and makes a difference in their own way. That's an important part of the culture we create when we play a kid's game with a senior's passion.

Other comments – My first year here, a player from Chicago told me, "I'd be dead today, if it weren't for softball." Now, more than a decade later, I understand fully what he was saying!

Name/Age – Jack Nesci, 72

Where Born? – Rochester, NY

Moved here from? – Rochester, NY

Job(s), Career – Xerox 10 years; owner of 3 video stores, 1981 - 1999

Leagues & Divisions played in – R3, RBL, CFL

Years Played - 20

Positions/Roles – SS, SF, 2B, manager R3/CFL, Board and V-P of CFL

Softball/Baseball/Other Sports Background – Baseball pitcher in grammar school and high school; pitcher in fast pitch softball for Kodak at 13 and 14 years of age; skiing; bowling.

Thoughts on softball here – The most organized softball since I played for Xerox and Kodak years ago.

Key players, teammates, & others important to you – Playing with Tom McGann, Wally Dias, and Ed Moriarity.

Other comments - The field conditions are outstanding.

Name/Age – Ron Nikstad, 66

Where Born? – Superior, WI

Moved here from? – Ham Lake, MN

Job(s), Career – Railroad Carman

Leagues & Divisions played in – R3, N3

Years Played - 6

Positions/Roles – Pitcher, Outfield

Softball/Baseball/Other Sports Background – Played Little League baseball; slow pitch softball, both unlimited arch and 6'-12' arch from age 18 to 37.

Thoughts on softball here – Wonderful leagues and diamonds to play on.

Key players, teammates, & others important to you – Woody Wood, who convinced me to sign up for Rec 3; Wayne Johnston, my first manager in Rec 3, who introduced me to Rec ball; Jerry Bullen, manager of my N-3 team had a big influence on my way of playing.

Name/Age – Bill Nisbet, 68

Where Born? – Columbus, OH

Moved here from? – Powell, OH

Job(s), Career – Health Food Inspector; Nationwide Insurance IT Manager

Leagues & Divisions played in – R3, CFL, N3, 68+

Years Played – 7

Positions/Roles - OF

Softball/Baseball/Other Sports Background – HS baseball; Urbana College baseball; softball in Columbus OH – 40 years; Columbus OH Softball Hall of Fame – 2015.

Thoughts on softball here – I love the length of the seasons and the re-drafting of rosters every season.

Key players, teammates, & others important to you – Ed Demaio, Ed Krisha, Ed Haith, Scott Marshall, Ron Nikstad.

Other comments – I've met a lot of wonderful people; played with and against very talented players. Regardless of age, I love the camaraderie of softball in this community.

Author's Note – Bill actually played high school baseball against my brother, Mike Kincaid, in Columbus, OH.

Name/Age – Bob Nyce, 73

Where Born? – Allentown, PA

Moved here from? – Northampton, PA

Job(s), Career – Corporate Tax Executive: Lehigh Portland Cement Co., Frick Co., Bethlehem Steel, Chrysler First, Inc. till 1989; PA State Representative 1990-96; PA Independent Regulatory Review Comm. 1997-2005; PA Auditor General candidate (R) 1996; Military – 1st Battalion, 3rd Infantry, The Old Guard, Arlington, VA, SSG E6, 1967-69.

Leagues & Divisions played in – R3, 68+, N3, CFL, Classic 70s; Veterans Tourney Div. 1/2/3 in 2017, 2018, and 2019 (won on Army team in 2017.) Also currently serve as Lead Evaluator for all Villages Softball, both men's and ladies programs.

Years Played – 2014 to present

Positions/Roles – mostly IF; coach/manager and umpire in 68+, R3, and N3

Softball/Baseball/Other Sports Background – Tennis all my life; no previous softball experience until evaluations here in 2013.

Thoughts on softball here – Great program run primarily by volunteers – announcers, scorekeepers, managers, umpires, Boards, evaluations of new players.

Key players, teammates, & others important to you – Players and Board members, umpires, and evaluators – all volunteers who keep things running smoothly are keys.

Other comments - Played for R3 Patriots, managed by Terry Jones for 7 seasons – great manager and fun to play with and for. Now enjoy playing for Jaguars and have played for Giants, Cowboys, Vikings, Seahawks, and Steelers. Div. 3 is not quite as intense as 1 and 2 and I really enjoy it. Have developed great friendships; in softball you must earn the respect of your fellow players. They know who is committed to the game. I'm now approaching age 74 and getting ready for the change to Div. 4 when necessary – ultimately my only goal is to keep playing as long as I can.

Name/Age – Richard Oliva, 72

Where Born? – Astoria, NY
Moved here from? – Long Island, NY

Job(s), Career – Retired from NY City Sanitation Dept.; 10 yrs w/Newsday (Long Island newspaper)

Leagues & Divisions played in – R3, N3, Veterans tournaments

Years Played – 2011 to present
Positions/Roles – SS - 8 yrs; now pitching

Softball/Baseball/Other Sports Background – Played sports all my life – baseball, basketball, hockey, football, bowling, stickball, softball, racquet ball and handball

Thoughts on softball here – It's like re-living my youth without the pressure of winning every game; now, it's more about having fun and meeting a lot of interesting people.

Key players, teammates, & others important to you – All are great, but you bond with a few – Kenny Anderson, Ron Goldman, George Van Ness, Jack Finn

Other comments – I also work the softball fields when I'm not playing. Duties include: lining the fields, cleaning the strike mats, putting out practice balls, setting up the scoreboards, checking the sound system; also trained in CPR and using the AED machine.

Name/Age – Ugo Perini, 74

Where Born? - Italy

Moved here from? - Connecticut

Job(s), Career – Worked for UPS

Leagues & Divisions played in – R3, N3, 68+, RBL

Years Played - 17

Positions/Roles – Outfield, Umpire

Softball/Baseball/Other Sports Background – Refereed and played soccer for 40 years; volleyball; pickleball.

Thoughts on softball here – It's the 'best pastime' for seniors.

Key players, teammates, & others important to you – There have been too many to remember them all.

Name/Age – John Plunkard, 69

Where Born? – Johnstown, PA

Moved here from? – Johnstown, PA

Job(s), Career – Accountant, Bethlehem Steel and Freight Car America

Leagues & Divisions played in – R1, R2, R3, N2, N3, CFL, Mid-Florida, Arena

Years Played - 16

Positions/Roles – Mostly 3B

Softball/Baseball/Other Sports Background – College baseball pitcher, 1970-73, Robert Morris University in Pittsburgh, PA

Thoughts on softball here – I go back to PA each summer. I've played softball in The Villages in the fall and winter seasons for 16 yrs. Each year I can't wait to get back and enjoy not only the game itself, but the multitude of men I call 'friend.'

Key players, teammates, & others important to you – Many, many.

Other comments – Good luck with your book, Dan.

Name/Age – Guy Poirier, 74

Where Born? – New Brunswick, Canada

Moved here from? – Still live in Canada; rent seasonally here

Job(s), Career – Corrections Canada

Leagues & Divisions played in – R3, N3, 68+

Years Played – 5 (during the winters)

Positions/Roles – 2B, SF, LCF

Softball/Baseball/Other Sports Background – softball, squash, racket ball, hockey

Thoughts on softball here – Super well organized; fields are excellent.

Key players, teammates, & others important to you – Managers – John Hoover, Jim Holloway; Players – Paul Hein, Paul Schaeffer

Name/Age – Ron Poux, 73

Where Born? – Meadville, PA

Moved here from? – Meadville, PA

Job(s), Career – Army Officer/Forward Air Observer in Vietnam; HVAC/Johnson Controls

Leagues & Divisions played in – R4, N4, RBL

Years Played – Going on 10 years

Positions/Roles – OF, Scorekeeper, Umpire

Softball/Baseball/Other Sports Background – Baseball, basketball, golf – pickleball & horseshoes.

Thoughts on softball here – This has to be the best Senior Softball organization to be found anywhere.

Key players, teammates, & others important to you – I've played with minor league baseball players, doctors, lawyers, West Point and Air Force Academy grads; I could go on and on. They all were great teammates. It makes you feel like we are one big family.

Other comments – Who would have thought that we would be playing softball in our 60s, 70s, and 80s? What a life!!

Name/Age – John T. Raines, 69

Where Born? – Montgomery, AL

Moved here from? – Destin, FL

Job(s), Career – Fire Chief, Montgomery, AL

Leagues & Divisions played in – R3, R4, N3, 68+

Years Played – 7 years

Positions/Roles – P, 1B, 3B, SF

Softball/Baseball/Other Sports Background – Baseball and softball

Thoughts on softball here – Great sport for 50 and older men, and 40 and older women.

Key players, teammates, & others important to you – Made too many friends to mention; best coaches I played for are Mark Olson and Wayne Johnston.

Other comments – I have been doing evaluations for seven years, to help get new people in the right divisions for their skill levels.

Name/Age – Ted Ramirez, 84

Where Born? – Hillside, NJ

Moved here from? – Miami, FL

Job(s), Career – U.S. Marine Corps 10 - yrs; Aircraft Mtce. – 29 yrs.

Leagues & Divisions played in – R2, N3, R3, CFL, Classics League, 68+, Veterans Tourneys

Years Played – Began in the fall of 2001; 'retired' a couple of years ago.

Positions/Roles – P, IF, Umpire, Manager, League Commissioner

Softball/Baseball/Other Sports Background – Sandlot football, baseball growing up. Started the football program and was head coach for nine years at a high school in Puerto Rico. Bowling while living in Puerto Rico, which included travel to tournaments in Panama, Columbia, and St. Thomas.

Thoughts on softball here – Great sport to make friends.

Key players, teammates, & others important to you – Too many to mention.

Other comments – Managed teams to two CFL championships. Pitched teams to championships in all leagues I played in. Was part of the organizing group that started the CFL in 2007.

Name/Age – William 'Bill' Reed, 74

Where Born? – Monongahela, PA

Moved here from? – Canonsburg, PA (also home town of Perry Como and Bobby Vinton)

Job(s), Career – Industrial Electrician – 40 yrs; two steel mills – ATI and Cyclops Steel

Leagues & Divisions played in – RBL, CFL, Arena, Classic 70s, N4 (my first year), R4, R3, R2 (last 4 yrs)

Years Played – Came here in 2009; played since 2012

Positions/Roles – LF, LCF, RCF, RF, C

Softball/Baseball/Other Sports Background - American Legion ball for Canonsburg; we played the Pirates farm team and beat them 4-2; they invited us to play again at Forbes Field, where they beat us twice, 5-3 and 4-3; CF fence was 457'. Played softball in the service 2 days/wk and for two years after I got out for local bar teams.

Thoughts on softball here – Well organized and with three seasons/yr on different teams, allows you to make a lot of new friends.

Key players, teammates, & others important to you – Kenny Atkinson and Charlie Clare. We make friendly little wagers for a lunch on most doubles or most extra base hits. I hold my own against these two good players. It's fun and gives us something to talk about or brag about. Many other great teammates; and manager John Ambrose. Good memory - in 2018 led league in doubles and extra base hits at age 72.

Name/Age – John Reedy, 76

Where Born? – Decatur, IL

Moved here from? – Decatur, IL

Job(s), Career – Farmer-20 yrs; drove 18-wheeler for 19 yrs; Lowe's delivery- 9 yrs.

Leagues & Divisions played in – R1, R2, N1/2, CFL, Arena, Classic, Mid-Florida

Years Played – 41 straight (3 mo.) seasons

Positions/Roles – SS, SF, 2B, OF

Softball/Baseball/Other Sports Background – HS baseball, basketball; fast pitch softball (pitcher) after HS; won IL State Tourney in 1968.

Thoughts on softball here – A great experience! Well organized. Good support from The Villages Rec Staff. Facilities are 1st class. Great way to make new friends and get some exercise.

Key players, teammates, & others important to you – I have met, played against, and with some very good players, some hall-of-famers. Carl McWilliams has the best throwing arm I ever saw!

Other comments – Would recommend Senior Softball to anyone who enjoys fun, exercise, competition, and good camaraderie.

Name/Age – Larry Rivellese, 74

Where Born? – Queens, NY
Moved here from? – New York
Job(s), Career – Union plumber

Leagues & Divisions played in – R3, R4, N3
Years Played – 17 years

Positions/Roles – Outfield as a player; (Larry also has sung the National Anthem and God Bless America for many of the Veterans Softball Tournaments.)

Softball/Baseball/Other Sports Background - HS baseball and football; softball later on in late teens and early 20s. .

Thoughts on softball here – It's great! It keeps you fit and you meet so many good people from all over the United States.

Key players, teammates, & others important to you – There are so many – players, managers, umpires, Board members. They make the leagues great.

Other comments – Author's Note – Larry has had quite a distinguished and long singing career. With a classical singing voice, Larry performs frequently at local churches, in shows at The Sharon, and was a regular at the Church on the Square, when that was going several years ago. He also sang and was interviewed on the Steve Harvey TV show a few years ago. Look up Larry on You Tube for more info.

Name/Age – Richard Rivers, 80

Where Born? – Springfield, MA

Moved here from? – Snowbird from Braintree, MA

Job(s), Career – Phys ed and science teacher, coach, mostly in Boston

Leagues & Divisions played in – R5

Years Played - 6

Positions/Roles – Mostly pitcher

Softball/Baseball/Other Sports Background – 70 years pickup basketball; 10 years Boston Teacher Softball League; 60+ years golf – 40 at Braintree, MA golf course.

Thoughts on softball here – The best place and most organized in the country. For older gents there is a softball team for you here. If you want, you probably could play softball 7 days a week.

Key players, teammates, & others important to you – Jim Anastasi is probably the best player and to me the best coach in R5; and then Terry Cole. Both were my coaches; kudos to each.

Other comments – Special thanks to Steve Hammond who runs open softball two days a week at Saddlebrook.

Name/Age – Joe Rocco, 76

Where Born? - PA

Moved here from? - PA

Job(s), Career – Military (Navy) Law Enforcement

Leagues & Divisions played in – R4, R5, N4, N5 and Veterans Tourney

Years Played - 12

Positions/Roles - SS

Softball/Baseball/Other Sports Background – Football and wrestling; never played softball until moving here.

Thoughts on softball here – Softball here has been unforgettable and tremendously enjoyable for me and numerous others.

Key players, teammates, & others important to you – Far too many players to mention; I've made many new friends playing softball.

Other comments – Softball is one of the best sports to play here. It keeps us active, which is important at our ages. One highlight is the Veterans Tournament every November. It honors veterans and promotes camaraderie among all of the service branches.

Name/Age – Gary Roth, 71

Where Born? – New Castle, PA

Moved here from? – New Castle, PA

Job(s), Career – Teacher; Home Contractor

Leagues & Divisions played in – R2, R3, N3 and the 70+ Div 1 travel team.

Years Played - 5

Positions/Roles – IF, OF

Softball/Baseball/Other Sports Background – HS football, basketball, baseball; college football at Edinboro State Univ., PA; softball in New Castle, PA

Thoughts on softball here – The facilities are amazing. I love how the divisions are leveled and the draft system.

Key players, teammates, & others important to you – Had a great relationship with Dan Kincaid. Enjoyed playing for Jack Nesci and Frenchie Le Tan; and playing with Tim Carroll, Steve Barton, and Jack Nagle.

Other comments – Recently moved to Parker, CO and because of playing in The Villages, I will play on three CO teams this spring and summer. If I hadn't moved, I was going to try and play R1. I had been going to some tournaments with those guys anyway.

Name/Age – Ray Saberg, 72

Where Born? – Staten Island, NY

Moved here from? – Charlottesville, VA

Job(s), Career – Accountant, Builder

Leagues & Divisions played in – R3, R2, N3, N2 RBL, 68+, CFL

Years Played – 2011 to present

Positions/Roles – OF, SS

Softball/Baseball/Other Sports Background – Played Senior Softball in Virginia for 4-5 years

Thoughts on softball here – Lots of fun and good guys to play with

Key players, teammates, & others important to you – Dan List, Steve Greenberg, Lindell Grigg, Dan Kincaid, Wayne Johnson, and many others.

Other comments – I've been on two R3 champions – Cardinals and Ravens; won R3 batting title one time with the Dolphins; won two RBL championships; and several N3 championships with Sunset Shores. Great fun!

Name/Age – Joe Sanchez, 77
Where Born? – Camaguey, Cuba
Moved here from? – Madison, CT

Job(s), Career – Political Science Professor at Adelphi Univ. in Garden City, NY; Attorney in Long Island, NY; Sports columnist in Reading, PA; Degrees from Columbia and Hofstra Universities, Albright College, and SUNY-Binghamton.

Leagues & Divisions played in – 65 seasons in R1, R2, R3, R4, and R5K; N 3, 4, and 5; 68+, RBL.
Years Played – 1998 - Present

Positions/Roles – LCF, SS, SF; President of original Softball Assoc.; Mgr. in Div. 2, 3, 4, and K5; Statistician in Div. 2; Umpire in D2, 3, and 4
Softball/Baseball/Other Sports Background – HS baseball, track, soccer; college cross-country

Thoughts on softball here – When I was in high school, Sports Illustrated ran a story on a softball league for 75-year old players in Florida. Even as a teenager, I thought that it would be wonderful to be playing the game at that age. And here I am!

Key players, teammates, & others important to you in – I have had the privilege to get to know dozens of outstanding individuals and players here. I will cite those that I met in my first few seasons: Lowell Thacker, Art Pelzer, Larry Liotta, Jack Augustine, Ron Thomas, Ron Dungan, Frank Hricay, and my very first manager, Roy Allen.

Name/Age – Vic Scalona, 67

Where Born? – Lynn, MA

Moved here from? – Lynn, MA

Job(s), Career - Firefighter

Leagues & Divisions played in – R4, R5

Years Played – Two seasons

Positions/Roles - OF

Softball/Baseball/Other Sports Background - Baseball, softball

Thoughts on softball here – Awesome program. Safety first. Fun and exercise as well.

Key players, teammates, & others important to you - Rick Proctor, Jim Anastasi, Rich Rivers, Dennis McMahon

Other comments – If softball interests you, it offers plenty of fun, making new friends, and socializing.

Name/Age – Larry Schiesel, 73

Where Born? - Michigan

Moved here from? - Michigan

Job(s), Career – Ret. US Army, US Treasury

Leagues & Divisions played in – N3, RBL

Years Played – 10 yrs in The Villages & 30 years prior

Positions/Roles - OF

Softball/Baseball/Other Sports Background -
Little League, Waterford Parks & Rec softball, HS
football and baseball, Ferris State College softball

Thoughts on softball here – I think players should
be re-evaluated every 5-7 years. Skills change and we
don't always want to admit it. A third party should
determine if you belong in a different division.

**Key players, teammates, & others important to
you** – Dan List, one of my evaluators and first
manager.

Name/Age – Bernie Schmidt, 69

Where Born? - Germany

Moved here from? – Menomonee Falls, WI

Job(s), Career – Supervisory in Printing Industry

Leagues & Divisions played in – R1, Travel Teams

Years Played – 2014 to present

Positions/Roles – OF, IF, C

Softball/Baseball/Other Sports Background –
Play on Handeland Flooring Travel Team, Milwaukee,
WI at the 70 major division this year.

Thoughts on softball here – Great competition,
great fields, great teammates

**Key players, teammates, & others important to
you** – Too many to single out, but some top notch
players on the national level.

Other comments – Also, I do Senior Olympics track
in the 50 and 100 meter races, as well as the Village
Games.

Name/Age – Dave Schultz, 60

Where Born? – Kankakee, IL

Moved here from? – McCordsville, IN

Job(s), Career – AIG Claims Rep.

Leagues & Divisions played in – R1, N1/2

Years Played – 5+

Positions/Roles - OF

Softball/Baseball/Other Sports Background – HS football, baseball, basketball; singles tennis and pickleball in The Villages

Thoughts on softball here – There are five Recreation divisions, which makes it possible for anyone who is interested in playing to compete. Also, there is a Board of Directors for each division, which is important.

Key players, teammates, & others important to you – The key people in my mind are the volunteers who make the programs possible. Thanks for your support!

Other comments – Well organized program from the start with evaluations, a draft; stats are kept on each player; and the end of season tourney is great.

Name/Age – Bob Seeber, 69

Where Born? – Grand Rapids, MI

Moved here from? - Michigan

Job(s), Career – Insurance Claims Adjuster

Leagues & Divisions played in – R3, N3, 68+, RBL

Years Played - 6

Positions/Roles – 2B, Manager

Softball/Baseball/Other Sports Background –
Football, baseball, softball

Thoughts on softball here – These are the best
fields and support that I've been involved with.

**Key players, teammates, & others important to
you** – Wally Dias, Manager in R3, was very helpful in
'navigating' through R3. Ron Pask taught me to play the
game and not be a spectator while in the field.

Name/Age – George Silk, 73

Where Born? – New Haven, CT

Moved here from? – North Haven, CT

Job(s), Career – New Haven police officer, 25 years; Milford, CT letter carrier, 11 years.

Leagues & Divisions played in – R3, N3, CFL, RBL
Years Played – 10-12 years (including a few surgeries)

Positions/Roles – OF, 1B, C. I now like to catch because it is equal distance from either dugout!

Softball/Baseball/Other Sports Background - I've umpired in N3, R3, RBL, and Div I women's league.

Thoughts on softball here – Softball is well organized in The Villages due to the vast amount of time put in by the volunteers. The fields are well maintained. The concession stands are great.

Key players, teammates, & others important to you – I couldn't even begin to name all of the great people that I've come in contact with; I wouldn't want to leave anyone out.

Other comments – I rented before buying a home. We moved here to play golf. I then went to watch a softball game. I looked at the players and said to myself 'if they can do it, so can I.' And I have felt like a kid again. There is a Disney World, but we have The Villages® community.

Name/Age – Peter Smith, 79   **Born** – Natick, MA

Moved here from? – Brewster, NY

Job(s), Career – Pro baseball pitcher 1961-65; then a math teacher and guidance counselor until 2002.

Leagues & Divisions played in – N1, N3, 68+

Years Played - 16

Positions/Roles – 1B, SF, manager, umpire

Softball/Baseball/Other Sports Background – Boston Red Sox organization; pitched in major leagues 1962-63. Started a triple play on 9/28/63 vs. the Los Angeles Angels.

Thoughts on softball here – I've enjoyed playing Neighborhood and 68+ softball; have made many friends by playing softball.

Key players, teammates, & others important to you – Best player I've played with here was Bob Wade, shortstop, but could play anywhere, a 5-tool player who hit .750 or better every season.

Other comments – I'd like to thank those on the Boards who run the leagues, especially Terry Cole for helping start the 68+ league and Matt Spanier for keeping it going the past 6-7 years. Thanks to Matt I've played organized ball in 9 decades from the 40s to now.

Name/Age – David Snyder, 82

Where Born? – Center Valley, PA

Moved here from? – Allentown, PA

Job(s), Career – Production Manager, Mack Trucks

Leagues & Divisions played in – Division 3 for a year; Division 4 for a season; the rest in R5K.

Years Played - 17

Positions/Roles – SF, 2B, OF

Softball/Baseball/Other Sports Background - Soccer

Thoughts on softball here – Great place; all ages have a chance to play.

Key players, teammates, & others important to you – Ed Mammele, 90 years and still playing; John Horwath played when he was 92; Armen Yeretzian played until 93; Jack Williamson, John Erb, Pete Modaff.

Other comments – I was Commissioner at Knudson for three years in the period when the field was completely re-done; new bathrooms added; and we played our games at Saddlebrook, Buffalo Glen, and Soaring Eagle.

Name/Age – Matt Spanier, 79

Where Born? – Hoboken, NJ

Moved here from? – Sayreville, NJ

Job(s), Career – Distribution and Transportation Mgmt. – Various companies

Leagues & Divisions played in – R3, N3, R4, CFL, RBL, Classics 70, 68+, Veterans Tourneys D3 and D4

Years Played – 2006 - present

Positions/Roles – OF, IF, P, C; manager in three different leagues; on Boards in two leagues; 68+ co-founder and commissioner.

Softball/Baseball/Other Sports Background – PAL and sandlot baseball as a kid; softball in grammar school, Navy, and leagues beginning in '68; softball tourneys for 20 years; 69+ years playing softball. Full contact touch football – 22 yrs; and no contact – 10 years. Industrial basketball – 10 yrs; league racquetball. Board, V-P, and manager, Sayreville Girls Softball.

Thoughts on softball here – Softball here is a player's dream; many fields; maintained at a high level. Players are from various backgrounds and states with one thing in common – playing softball and having fun – among friends.

Key players, teammates, & others important to you – Too many great players and individuals to choose from.

Name/Age – Rocky Spottswood, 66

Where Born? – Riverdale, MD

Moved here from? – Columbia, MD

Job(s), Career – Roofing; **Years Played** – Since 2014

Leagues & Divisions played in – R2, N2, CFL, Beef O' Brady's Tournament Team

Positions/Roles - OF, Manager of Orioles for 12 seasons and counting

Softball/Baseball/Other Sports Background – HS baseball, then softball until age 41. Then started managing teams in MD, including for my twin girls who are still playing today in MD.

Thoughts on softball here – Can't be any better! Field conditions are great and organization is incredible. The people I've met are wonderful. I love it!

Key players, teammates, & others important to you – My good friend Charlie Clare. Teammates are too numerous to mention. Every season is different, due to the draft. Also a shout out to Frankie Murth, who still plays at age 82.

Other comments – Wouldn't change a thing. Love the 'drafts', the friendships, and the challenge on the field every day.

Name/Age – Doug St. Andrews, 66

Where Born? – Schenectady, NY

Moved here from? – Schenectady, NY

Job(s), Career – GE/Pepsi Cola, Schenectady County

Leagues & Divisions played in – Neighborhood 3, Rec 3, RBL, CFL

Years Played – 6 years

Positions/Roles – Outfield/Manager/Umpire

Softball/Baseball/Other Sports Background – High school baseball, football, wrestling

Thoughts on softball here – A great way to meet other Villagers and new lifetime friends.

Key players, teammates, & others important to you – Bruce Thompson, my first manager here, set the bar high on how to become a good manager.

Other comments – Dan Austin is 83 years old and still playing; an incredibly nice guy and still a great player.

Name/Age – Terry Sullivan, 74

Where Born? – Akron, OH

Moved here from? – Uniontown, OH

Job(s), Career – 46 years in the grocery retail business; went from carryout boy to store manager.

Leagues & Divisions played in – R5, R4, N5, 68+

Years Played - 10

Positions/Roles – OF, IF (mostly SS), pitcher

Softball/Baseball/Other Sports Background -HS football, basketball, baseball; summer baseball Akron; church softball later; senior softball in OH, then Altamont Springs, FL, and now in The Villages.

Thoughts on softball here – We moved here because of the first class softball facilities, friendly atmosphere, and organization. We old men even get our names and photos in the local newspaper sometimes!

Key players, teammates, & others important to you – Great teammates; drafting new teams each season means getting to know everyone

Other comments – A former baseball teammate caught one of Nolan Ryan's no-hitters; played HS basketball with future NBA player, Bill Turner; and played HS football against Larry Csonka and got two front teeth knocked out that game.

Name/Age – Bill Taylor, 82

Where Born? – Honaker, VA

Moved here from? – Brandywine, MD

Job(s), Career – Wholesale Bakery Business

Leagues & Divisions played in – R4, R5, N3, 68+, RBL

Years Played – 2007 - present

Positions/Roles – Player/Manager, 2B, 1B, OF; managed RBL Ripkens team for 10 years; managed 68+ Cobras team for six years.

Softball/Baseball/Other Sports Background - A little golf here and there, as well as softball

Thoughts on softball here – Involved with RBL since 2008. My wife Jeri began helping behind the scenes in 2010 and then primarily ran the league from 2012 -2017, until Jack Nagle and Wayne Grunewald took over.

Key players, teammates, & others important to you - Dan List

Other comments – Jeri had no softball skills, but we needed help running the scoreboards and her input took off from there. Her auditing skills helped her put things together and keep track of things.

Name/Age – Rick Valdes, 78

Where Born? – Havana, Cuba

Moved here from? – Miami, FL

Job(s), Career – Advertising, Sales

Leagues & Divisions played in – Div.'s 1, 2, 3, & 4

Years Played – Player and/or manager for 20 years

Positions/Roles – Infield; manager since 2009

Softball/Baseball/Other Sports Background – Baseball in high school and U.S. Air Force; All-Star SS for Pacific Air Forces; fast pitch softball at Hancock Field in NY

Thoughts on softball here – Absolutely great! However, a lot of players get mis-evaluated either higher or lower than they should be

Key players, teammates, & others important to you – Too many to name; all helped create good memories for me

Other comments – Looking forward to this book; a story that needs to be told; all of us old grandfather types still running around looking forward to the next game. What a way to leave this life!!

Name/Age – Jim Vigliarolo, 67

Where Born? – Brooklyn, NY

Moved here from? – Valley Stream, NY

Job(s), Career – U.S. Postal Service – 35 years; Manager, Distribution Operations.

Leagues & Divisions played in – N3, RBL

Years Played – 11+ years

Positions/Roles – IF/OF

Softball/Baseball/Other Sports Background - Softball in NY – Postal Service Leagues; Neighborhood Leagues in Brooklyn and Valley Stream.

Thoughts on softball here – Playing softball in The Villages is enjoyable. Very organized and well thought out for safety.

Key players, teammates, & others important to you – When I first started playing in August 2008, Rick Montroy was my manager. He was very helpful in getting me involved.

Other comments – I have lived in the Village of Amelia since July 2008. Since they have no N3 league in our village, I have played with many different neighborhood teams. Each team has been great in allowing me to play for them.

Name/Age – Ray Walters, 76

Where Born? - Philadelphia

Moved here from? – New Jersey

Job(s), Career – Sales Mgr. for Chemical Co.

Leagues & Divisions played in – R3, N3, Classics, CFL, FL Half Century

Years Played - 10

Positions/Roles – SF, OF, Ump, Mgr, Commissioner

Softball/Baseball/Other Sports Background - High School football and baseball

Thoughts on softball here – The Parks & Rec Dept. does a wonderful job of running all the softball programs. It's a great way to stay young in retirement.

Key players, teammates, & others important to you – All volunteers who ump, score, manage, and work on the Boards are special. One who stands out is Wally Dias, who played, managed, and was Commissioner in R3 and D3 for about 9 years. He still creates game schedules for us.

Other comments – If it wasn't for the softball program here, I would probably be a couch potato.

Name/Age – Mike Weiss, 75

Where Born? – Brooklyn, NY

Moved here from? – Queens, NY

Job(s), Career – Hotel Manager

Leagues & Divisions played in – R4, R5, 68+, N4, N5

Years Played - 12

Positions/Roles – SS, 3B, 2B, manager

Softball/Baseball/Other Sports Background – All sports until age 21

Thoughts on softball here – Love it!

Key players, teammates, & others important to you – Terry Cole, Kirby Campanella, and about 1,000 various ballplayers.

Name/Age – Doug White, 64

Where Born? – New London, CT
Moved here from? – New Hampshire
Job(s), Career – Engineering Management for Telecom and Cellular Telecom
Leagues/Divisions – R3, N3, RBL **Years Played** - 5
Positions/Roles – 1B, SF, several other positions
Softball/Baseball/Other Sports Background – Little League, Babe Ruth, JV high school baseball. HS Target Rifle team, captain for two years and won back to back CT state championships.
Thoughts on softball here – One of the reasons I wanted to live here, to play ball at a competitive level again. The players are great people and want to have fun while still playing to win. The five evaluation skill levels are important in order to match players at levels suitable for one another.
Key players, teammates, & others important to you – I'm impressed by all the volunteers who make things run so well – the umps, managers, scorekeepers, board members. Most city leagues elsewhere have paid umps, which to me, takes some of the camaraderie out of the game.
Other comments – I enjoy volunteering as a computer scorekeeper for the R3 league, which I think is the only league doing that. We score the details of each game and record the plays; hit position; hit type; and then submit the score sheets to the local newspaper. Managers can access every player's hit location, 'spray' diagram, and other batting stats to get an idea of defensive strategy against each batter.

Name/Age – Dave Williams, 71

Where Born? – Herculaneum, MO

Moved here from? – St. Louis, MO

Job(s), Career – St. Louis Metro Police Dept.

Leagues & Divisions played in – R3, 68+, RBL

Years Played – 2013 - Present

Positions/Roles – OF, 1B

Softball/Baseball/Other Sports Background -
St. Louis Metro Police Softball League

Thoughts on softball here – It's a great place to live.
You can play softball all year long if you choose.

**Key players, teammates, & others important to
you** – One person who stands out in my opinion, who
is a key player and manager, as well as an inspiration to
all Division 3 players, is Doug St. Andrews. He steps up
in any situation he is confronted with and offers his
experience to all those beginning their softball careers
here.

Other comments – You meet interesting players
from all over the country and world.

Name/Age – Woody Wood, 67

Where Born? – Alexandria, VA

Moved here from? – Alexandria, VA

Job(s), Career – Lineman, postal service

Leagues & Divisions played in – R3, R4, N3, RBL, CFL

Years Played - 8

Positions/Roles – OF, Manager in RBL & CFL, Umpire

Softball/Baseball/Other Sports Background - None

Thoughts on softball here – Enjoy the camaraderie with other players- 'A great time had by all'

Key players, teammates, & others important to you – Bill Taylor got me started in RBL and Dan List was just the best in promoting softball. Jerry Bullen, Mr. Softball in Neighborhood of Buttonwood. His quote, "Score early, score often."

Other comments – The Villages® community has a great sports program that fits just about everyone!

Name/Age – Kenneth Wykrent, 69

Where Born? – Detroit, MI

Moved here from? – Dearborn, MI

Job(s), Career – Marathon Petroleum Co.

Leagues & Divisions played in – R3, RBL, 68+, N3

Years Played - 7

Positions/Roles – OF, 1B, 2B, 3B, C, announcing, scorekeeping

Softball/Baseball/Other Sports Background –
Baseball as a youth, ice hockey, some softball on the company team, recreational golf, coached youth hockey

Thoughts on softball here – It's the greatest thing! Never thought at this age I'd be playing ball and running the bases. However, I was plagued by the normal injuries that new players have. I needed pinch runners and they were older than me! But now we warm up, stretch, put on our hats, sunglasses, and gloves, sit a little taller, and feel like we're 19 years old again.

Key players, teammates, & others important to you – In addition to the players there are the volunteer coaches, umpires, stat keepers, announcers, board members, concession stand folks, wives and cheering friends. The grounds keepers meticulously maintain the fields. Great facilities!

Other comments – We play for exercise, competition, camaraderie, and fun. We all make mistakes out there and no one is harder on us than we are on our own selves. But when we do make a great play; stop a hard hit grounder; make a terrific catch in the outfield; get a base hit or sometimes even a home run – what a rush!! Hey, we're old and it's great to win a game. But I'd say we're all winners by just coming out to play.

(Women's Player Bio's - Alphabetical List)

Name/Age – Madelaine 'Tiny' Cazel, 82

Where Born? – Chicago, IL

Moved here from? – Arlington, IL

Job(s), Career – Always had a paper route as a kid; played 16" Chicago ball at the Rec Center playground

Leagues & Divisions played in – Rec ball since 2001; Vixens, Golden Gals, Tri-County

Years Played – 20 years; began travel ball in 2001

Positions/Roles – 3B, SF, LF

Softball/Baseball/Other Sports Background - Track and Field; Running – 50M and 100M; hold various senior records in javelin and discus; also do shot put.

Thoughts on softball here – Softball is a great activity here. I've enjoyed playing these last 20 years, including state and national tournaments and other travel tourneys, with all of my teammates.

Key players, teammates, & others important to you – First travel team, the Vixens, with Coach Al Mahar; John Rohan & Pam Henry – Rec Dept; players – Avis Vaught, Aileen Laing, Darleen Hedrick, Marie Panza, Jan Washburn, and many more.

Other comments – Started playing at Knudson in 2000 with Betty Josephson; 15-20 ladies showed up. In 2003 the Tri-County Golden Ladies started which continued to add teams from outside communities. That grew to the Tri-County League, which has kept growing.

Name/Age – Karen Coll, 73

Where Born? – Lawton, OK

Moved here from? – Altamonte Springs, FL

Job(s), Career – Dept. of Defense/U.S. Army Research Institute for the Behavioral and Social Sciences-38 yrs; U.S. Army Medical Specialist, Vietnam era – 2 yrs and VA Hospital – 1 yr.

Leagues & Divisions played in – Ladies Div.1/2/3

Years Played - 20

Positions/Roles – Mostly P; some other IF

Softball/Baseball/Other Sports Background – Tennis #1; softball; pickleball

Thoughts on softball here – With all of the fields we have, it makes playing here so easy. Precautions are taken with the evaluations to place players in the proper divisions for safety reasons. Safety is a priority with the Boards in all Divisions.

Key players, teammates, & others important to you – Donna Levery, Avis Vaught, Ellen Pearce, and all the volunteers in keeping up with softball and making it so special here. Wendy Burns is our photographer.

Other comments – Danny Jacobs and his crew are the best; easy to work with; and helping to ensure the Veterans Tourney is handled with pride and respect.

Name/Age – Jo Cool, 65

Where Born? - Missouri

Moved here from? - Missouri

Job(s), Career – Owned Trash Co.

Leagues & Divisions played in - 6

Years Played – 30 yrs

Positions/Roles – SS, LF, 1B

Softball/Baseball/Other Sports Background -

Thoughts on softball here – What a blessing it is to step onto these gorgeous fields and play.

Key players, teammates, & others important to you – So many to mention. My late husband had Alzheimer's/Lewy Body Dementia. These girls would take turns watching him so that I could play.

Other comments – The players' friendships on the field is one thing, but it carries off the fields, too.

Name/Age – Sue Dahl, 63

Where Born? – Eau Claire, WI

Moved here from? – Chippewa Falls, WI

Job(s), Career -

Leagues & Divisions played in – Tri-County 1 & 2, Rec. 2

Years Played - 6

Positions/Roles – SF, manager, asst. manager

Softball/Baseball/Other Sports Background – After HS, started playing slow pitch softball – Women's and Co-Ed; bowling; pickleball

Thoughts on softball here – Women's softball continues to get better; by expanding to a third division, it is a better game.

Key players, teammates, & others important to you – Jane Bakke started me as an assistant manager in my second season and that helps you really get to know all the women. I have enjoyed it.

Other comments – I have made so many friends; and it came at a time in my life when I really needed it.

Name/Age – Sis Dueholm, 64

Born? – Ilion, NY   **Moved from?** – Sheboygan, WI

Job(s), Career – Farming, Grocery Clerk, Bookkeeper Loan Accountant; County Executive Director for USDA for 26 years

Leagues & Divisions played in – Ladies R2, N5, and Tri-County Ladies   **Years Played** – 8

Positions/Roles – Most positions except P and SS; and serve on two softball Boards.

Softball/Baseball/Other Sports Background – I grew up with four brothers and we played sports every day. I played league softball in my 20s.

Thoughts on softball here – I ask myself every day 'how can I be so lucky as to live in this community and play softball at such wonderful facilities'? Well, I worked hard my whole life and always treated people with respect and kindness. I suppose living here is my reward. I just love softball and living here.

Key players, teammates, & others important to you – The list is too long, but includes players, managers, scorekeepers, evaluators, umpires, Board members, ground crews, and Rec Dept.

Other comments – Spend most of my time on things related to softball, such as practice and batting lessons. The friendships are very important.

Name/Age – BJ Durkin, 77

Where Born? – Dayton, OH

Moved here from? – Centerville, OH

Job(s), Career – Kettering School System, Anderson Security System, Continental Cablevision; Accounting

Leagues & Divisions played in – Ladies Rec Leagues, starting at Knudson; Neighborhood Co-Ed; Travel teams

Years Played – 16 yrs.

Positions/Roles – 2B, C, SF, Mgr for 24 seasons

Softball/Baseball/Other Sports Background – HS field hockey, basketball, softball, bowling, golf

Thoughts on softball here – Softball is my passion. I have met many nice people over the years

Key players, teammates, & others important to you – My idol was Bert Burk who played till her mid-80's; Helen Weslowski helped with my playing mechanics; Ellen Pearce taught a great clinic.

Other comments – I encourage everyone to try softball. It's great fun! Some new residents, who never played before, have found a new passion.

Name/Age – Midge Ferraro, 71

Where Born? – Troy, NY
Moved here from? – Long Island, NY
Job(s), Career - Teacher

Positions/Roles/Years Played – This is my 50th year of coaching softball

Softball/Baseball/Other Sports Background - Played college softball; played regional and national slow pitch softball

Thoughts on softball here – Will continue working with administrators and others to develop a better public platform for women's softball. Over 50,000 women live here, but only 100+ are playing softball. So, we're missing a few!

Key players, teammates, & others important to you – Avis Vaught, Evie Hayes, Kathy Tittle, Chris Terrill, Alice Terrill, Karen Learn, Chris Evans, Beth Bullock

Other comments – Softball is a team sport; but, more so than in most other team sports, the individual is highlighted. The way an individual executes things is showcased in the minds of fans, players, and coaches – until the next pitch! That places immense psychological pressure on the player to perform better or to continue performing at a high level. The need to let the last play go and concentrate on the next play is the hardest skill to teach.

Name/Age – Jane Girotti, 74

Where Born? – Philadelphia, PA
Moved here from? – Langhorne, PA
Job(s), Career – Proprietor-flower shop and private mail center; Admin Asst/Office Mgr-Staffing Agency
Leagues & Divisions – Ladies D2, D3; N4, N5; 75+ tourneys/Golden Gals   **Years Played** – 10 yrs.
Positions/Roles – OF, LCF – Rec; various in N4/5; served on Ladies D2 Board for two terms; manpower for N4/5; N5 board at present and manpower N5.
Softball/Baseball/Other Sports Background – Played varsity softball and field hockey in HS; played ladies softball 1968-72; coached and managed many girls softball teams, including Girls 18/under Traveling Team; first female baseball coach/mgr for Lower Southampton Athletic Assoc.; V-P Girls Athletic Assoc – NE High School.

Thoughts on softball here – Appreciate all the levels offered. The success of the programs amazes me – by all volunteers. I have enjoyed growing the N5 program into a true Co-Ed League.

Key players, teammates, & others important to you – Many friends in softball. Some are Dave Bigelow, Mike Heck, Avis Vaught, Liz Sinicropi, Ellen Pearce, Chris Evans, Sis Dueholm, Bruce Carlson, Doug St. Andrews, and many more.

Other comments – My husband also plays. Truthfully, I enjoy watching his games almost as much as I enjoy playing. We have formed many friendships from all Divisions. Softball, in general, is one big family. We all have a love for the game.

Name/Age – Darlene Hedrick, 76
Where Born? – Riverside, CA

Moved here from? - Virginia

Job(s), Career – Paint Manager

Leagues & Divisions played in – Rec 1, 2, 3; Neighborhood; Tri-County; Tournaments; Men's D5.

Years Played – In The Villages since 2005; 48 yrs total

Positions/Roles – Mostly OF, but all positions at one time or another.

Softball/Baseball/Other Sports Background – Bowling and softball

Thoughts on softball here – Great softball fields. I moved here to be able to play all year long. If not for all the softball, I most likely would not have moved to this community.

Key players, teammates, & others important to you – So many great ones that I wouldn't want to leave anyone out.

Other comments – I love playing softball with everyone.

Name/Age – Shirley Jones, 72
Where Born? – Burlington, WI
Moved here from? – WI/IL
Job(s), Career – Cosmetologist, homemaker, wife, mother, bank teller

Leagues & Divisions played in/Years Played – Tri-County Travel Team 1997-2020, Ladies Rec League 1998-2020, Div 3 N'hood player/coach 2001-2015
Positions/Roles – First woman on the Softball Advisory Board; player/manager on 1st Ladies Rec teams; played Div 1,2,3 at Knudson, Saddlebrook, Buffalo Glen, and Soaring Eagle.

Softball/Baseball/Other Sports Background – Downhill skier; NASTAR Gold & Silver Medals; FL and national Senior Games- track, field, softball.

Thoughts on softball here – I'm so happy to have been a part of Ladies Softball from the very beginning and watch it grow. I've met some wonderful people over the years and continue to make more new friends every season.

Key players, teammates, & others important to you – John Rohan, Pam Henry, Scott Grimes – Rec Dept; Penny Zielinski, Avis Vaught, Aileen Laing, Bert Burk, Betty Josephson, Joyce Quintel

Other comments – One of 4 women still playing softball after 20 years including Phyllis Ryden, Barb Wheelus, Denise Emch. 15-year volunteer for Sertoma Baseball Camp for deaf and hearing impaired children.

Name/Age – Aileen Laing, 76

Where Born? – Fairfield, CT

Moved here from? – South FL

Job(s), Career - SunTrust

Leagues & Divisions played in – Div 1, 2, 3

Years Played - 20

Positions/Roles – National Tourney, 1B

Softball/Baseball/Other Sports Background -
Played basketball in high school

Thoughts on softball here – The best!

**Key players, teammates, & others important to
you** - In 2002, we created a National tournament team
of the ladies from here. We were called the Vixens.

Other comments – Began playing in the 50s bracket,
then 55, 60, and 65. We played all over the country and
were undefeated for several years. I am proud to have
been a part of its creation along with my husband,
Coach Al Mahar.

Name/Age – Barb Lukens, 74

Where Born? – Providence, RI
Moved here from? - Connecticut
Job(s), Career – Cable TV Executive, Realtor

Leagues & Divisions played in – R1, R2, Tri-County Ladies, Golden Gals travel teams (65, 70, 75s), Neighborhood league
Years Played – 2011 - 2020
Positions/Roles – 3B, 2B, 1B, C, Manager

Softball/Baseball/Other Sports Background – Open League fast pitch (late 60s – mid 70s). Have played volleyball, basketball, bocce, water volleyball and competed in track & field (discus, shot put, javelin). Like to hike and kayak.

Thoughts on softball here – Softball was always my first love; I was so pleased to be able to play again after 30-35 yrs. I appreciate the opportunity so much and have met so many fun people and good players.

Key players, teammates, & others important to you – Midge Ferraro, Avis Vaught, Julie Bradley, Chris Evans, Beth Quesnel, George Allman and all of the umpires. Many, many players in all leagues.

Other comments – Those of us who play softball here are a community in and of itself – a support group for all of us and our families.

Name/Age – Gloria Tallee Miller, 75

Where Born? – Tallahassee, FL
Moved here from? – Long Beach, CA

Job(s), Career – Teacher – math, health, and science: trig, geometry, algebra, biology, chemistry, physics. Coached softball, basketball, cheerleaders, drill team. Bookkeeper.
Leagues & Divisions played in – Rec.1,2,3; Tri-County Golden Gals; Travel team; Neighborhood men's.

Years Played – Total 23 and 7 in The Villages

Positions/Roles – LF, SF, 1B, 2B, 3B, SS, P; coach, manager, sponsor

Softball/Baseball/Other Sports Background – Started playing softball at age 52. Swimming, bowling, basketball, golf, roller skating.

Thoughts on softball here – It is a wonderful opportunity for any skill level to be able to play and practice. We also have a 'prayer' group in place to assist with those kinds of needs for players.

Key players, teammates, & others important to you – Tiny Cazel, Carol Courter, Marie Panza, Avis Vaught, Linda Snell, Barb Lukens, Beth Bullock, and coaches Midge Ferraro, Chris Evans

Other comments – 15 X national/world champion; 10 X Sr Olympic Champion; one of the first Women's world champion teams.

Name/Age – Pam Napoletano, 67
Where Born? – St. Louis, MO
Moved here from? – Huntsville, AL
Job(s), Career – Contracting Officer for U.S. Air Force and NASA
Leagues & Divisions played in – Women's D1
Years Played–14; **Positions/Roles** – SS, 3B, Mgr.
Softball/Baseball/Other Sports Background – I played recreational softball growing up; and in college and the Air Force. Since moving here, I play Rec League, tournaments, pickleball, and golf.
Thoughts on softball here – I began at Knudson in 2006. Since then, the women's leagues have grown from one to three. In 2012 we entered the first all-women's team in the Veterans Tournament. In 2013 we won our first game in that tourney. In 2018 we made it to the championship game, but lost. In 2019 we won the D5 championship of the Thomas E. Kennedy Memorial Veterans Day Tournament.

Key players, teammates, & others important to you – I wouldn't have started playing softball here if I hadn't stopped by Betty Josephson's practice at Knudson and then attended Midge Ferraro's clinics at the field. I haven't stopped playing since. I have played with many great players along the way on both Rec and Tournament teams and made many great friends.

Other comments – Softball here is all about the camaraderie. I also want to thank all of the volunteers that step up to make the program what it is today. I encourage everyone to step in and volunteer to keep the program growing.

Name/Age – Cathy Norris, 66

Where Born? – Bangor, Maine

Moved here from? – Dunedin, FL

Job(s), Career – Rec & Parks field – worked summer camps in Brewer, ME during HS and college; Rec Director for Searsport, ME; golf course near Clearwater, FL; Rec supervisor for FL Sheriff's Youth Ranch in Clearwater; City of Dunedin, FL Rec & Parks for 23 yrs; then 8 yrs as Manager of Marion Co. Parks & Rec; retired now, but still work part-time at Tierra Del Sol.

Leagues & Divisions played in – N4 Belvedere, then with Liberty Park; served on N4 Board for 7+ yrs; after retiring from full-time jobs began playing Ladies Rec 1; also served on that Board.

Years Played – Since around 2008-09

Positions/Roles – Mainly pitcher; in N4 with Belvedere played SS; sometimes in ladies tourneys have played OF.

Softball/Baseball/Other Sports Background – In HS was fast-pitch pitcher; played in many slow pitch leagues after HS, both ladies and co-ed; in HS and college played basketball, field hockey, and volleyball (my college did not have softball.) Played tournament softball summers in Maine until moving to FL in 1982. Did not play tourney ball again until my early 50s with the Silver Bullets, based out of The Villages®, which is how I came to learn about this community. Later played with the Vixens and now on Sunny Beaches, all within the various age brackets for the travel teams. Also began co-ed softball again when I moved here.

Thoughts on softball here – When you think about it, there isn't a place anywhere that provides the level of softball and the caliber of facilities that we have. The number of men and women players at five different levels is astounding.

Key players, teammates, & others important to you – Chris Evans truly loves this game. Though she is not playing anymore, she does coach and has always umpired. She just loves softball. When she played she always got so excited and pumped up that I always enjoyed being on the field with her.

I first played N4 with Ella Redpath on Belvedere and she has such a life spirit about her – always cheering and pumping up the team. When she went through a serious health situation I truly believe her positive attitude was a key in beating the odds. She fought thru that and came back to play again and be part of our teams. It was a miracle to watch and I will always enjoy my time playing softball with Ella.

Name/Age – Marie L. Panza, 78

Where Born? – Berea, OH

Moved here from? – Parma, OH

Job(s), Career – Vocational School, & bus driver

Leagues & Divisions played in – Started at Knudson in 2004 on D4 teams; Golden Gals; began playing 'national' ball at age 64; still play on 80's national team from The Villages.

Years Played – 16 years
Positions/Roles – 1B, 3B

Softball/Baseball/Other Sports Background – Never had ball in my youth, but was in a 'housewives' league when my children were in school.

Thoughts on softball here – We are on the softball map because of the Golden Gals. We have been the best in the USA thanks to our coach, Midge Ferraro.

Key players, teammates, & others important to you – Evie Hayes, who played for the Hialeah Dots and Golden Gals; Tiny Cazel; Lois Borie, and Marcia Halverson (from MN) – on the 80's team.

Other comments – Have won many tournaments in Pittsburgh, Cleveland, Louisville, San Francisco, Houston, Albuquerque, and in Utah.

Name/Age – Ella Redpath, 73

Where Born? - Scotland

Moved here from? – Baltimore, MD

Job(s), Career – Registered Nurse

Leagues & Divisions played in – Ladies D 1,2,3; Tournament teams; N4,5; Men's D5 several summers

Years Played - 13

Positions/Roles – Player, Ump, Manager, Board

Softball/Baseball/Other Sports Background – Track & Field Senior Games; pickleball

Thoughts on softball here – The chance of a lifetime to play a new sport (for me) at such a high level of competitiveness; open to all levels of skill.

Key players, teammates, & others important to you – Midge Ferraro, Avis Vaught, Josie LaNasa, Betty Josephson (who was my mentor in 2006 when I showed up at Knudson, green as grass), Cathy Norris, Denise Emsch, B.J. Durkin, Aileen Laing, Al Mahar.

Other comments – All of the individuals listed above played a huge part in my enjoyment of the game. Each coached and encouraged me with tips and many hours of practice. Josie was my roommate on travel tournament teams.

Name/Age – Linda Soos, 79

Where Born? – Charleston, WV

Moved here from? – Salisbury, NC

Job(s), Career – Entrepreneur – Owned and operated 3 beauty salons for 25 yrs in MI; BS from Eastern MI Univ, taught HS for 10 yrs.

Leagues & Divisions played in – Rec 1,2,3; Golden Gals and Tri-County.

Years Played–2007–present.

Positions/Roles - P

Softball/Baseball/Other Sports Background – Playground ball (women didn't have school sports) and horse riding; now also play pickleball and golf.

Thoughts on softball here – Wonderful! Nice people, great friends, keeps me healthy. Being able to switch divisions as skill levels change is nice.

Key players, teammates, & others important to you – With Golden Gals played tourneys in UT, TX, TN, GA, SC, VA, Ft. Myers, and Tampa. Two great coaches – Midge Ferraro and Chris Evans.

Other comments – I was 66 when I started in D1; later went to D2; I've had back surgery and knee replacement and now play D3. I'm blessed to live here, staying active and healthy.

Name/Age – Avis L. Vaught, 73

Where Born? – Miami, FL

Moved here from? – Newark, DE

Job(s), Career – Taught Health, Drivers Ed – Grades 10-12 and Phys Ed Grades K-12; High School Coach in volleyball, softball, basketball, soccer, indoor track, and tennis; Coach-Olympic Development Program – soccer. These were all during my 25 years in Delaware.

Leagues & Divisions played in – Rec 1, 2; State Senior Games; Tri-County; Tournament/Travel teams - Vixens, Diamonds, Golden Gals

Years Played – 2005 - present

Positions/Roles – Softball Advisory Board; Rec 1 Board; Evaluation Committee; player, manager, umpire, scorekeeper; skills clinics for ladies; leader for indoor volleyball program.

Softball/Baseball/Other Sports Background – Miami Dots (Marlinettes) Women's Softball Team, 1965-69; Miami-Dade JC/ Florida State Univ – golf, volleyball, track (1969 All- American hurdler); Little League baseball 1958 – pitcher; Special Olympics Track coach; Drill Team Director at North Marion HS 1972.

Thoughts on softball here – The Villages® Recreation Dept has created a safe environment for the senior population to continue playing our country's number one favorite pastime game – softball. This is a game you can play from age 7 to 97. Locally, we have not only the recreation leagues, but the opportunity for more competitive play with the tournament teams.

Key players, teammates, & others important to you – Midge Ferraro assisted with benchmark guidelines for Ladies Softball evaluations; Tiny Cazel has been a mentor in track; Kathy Tittle provides leadership in team management; Leslie Young and Amy Hennon with statistical skills; Betty Josephson for love of the game; Pam Henry assisting with the beginning of our ladies program.

Other comments – We are very fortunate to have Florida weather 12 months a year permitting our residents the opportunity to be on the 'diamond' every day. Residents coming from everywhere have that personal drive – their 'love of the game' – that brings them to the fields. This game has created 'softball families' within our community.

Name/Age – Penny Zielinski, 67

Where Born? – Upstate NY
Moved here from? – South Carolina

Job(s), Career – Registered Nurse

Leagues & Divisions played in – Tri-County, R1, N2, N1, N4. Travel Teams-Village Vixens, Silver Bullets, Sunny Beaches (Clearwater). In 2013 got picked up by Jolico out of MI. We play all over and are one of the top teams in the nation – number one the past three years.

Yrs Played – 20   **Positions/Roles** – OF, manager

Softball/Baseball/Other Sports Background - When I moved here in 1999, I was only 47 years old and they let me play in the Tri-County League. They all called me 'the kid.' Those were the days. I played Tri-County for nine years.

Thoughts on softball here – Around 2002 we started playing Villages Rec League. Played on men's teams in Neighborhood League. Our ladies travel teams did quite well in various tournaments.

Key players, teammates, & others important to you – Many, many fine players and friends.

Other comments – I still play Ladies Rec 1 and Neighborhood 4, but unfortunately I had rotator cuff surgery in November 2019 and I'm currently on injured reserve.

VI. POSTSCRIPT

So, there you have it – a short overview of softball in The Villages® community, as well as Bio's for a cross-section of players from every league here.

This has been a time-consuming task, much more involved than I initially thought it would be. When I write a book of fiction, I just write what comes into my mind or in a direction that I decide to follow. For a book like this, however, gathering all of the information and talking with so many people is a whole different ballgame. It was definitely a challenge – so many trips to the softball fields to talk with folks; so many phone calls and the inevitable phone tag. And to try and verify things as much as possible within a reasonable time period; and finally to put it all together so that it flows fairly well. Let's just say that out of the 11 books I have written, this has not been the easiest one to complete.

As for the player Bio's, I have included approximately five percent of the softball players here. There was no particular rhyme or reason as to how I determined who to feature; other than I wanted to include at least five players, men and women both, from every division and league here, including travel/tournament teams. I wanted to have representation from long-time players, newer players, and those in between. So I visited the fields numerous times, explaining what I was doing, and distributing questionnaires for players to fill out and return to me.

The questionnaires began coming back, some electronically and some by mail, and some had a type of writing with which I was not familiar (just kidding, sort of.) I had to decipher as best I could, try to make follow-up calls to find out what the writer was trying to say; and then re-type everything into a consistent format.

Once I began to tally up the forms from players and which leagues they play in or have played in, I saw that I had a few gaps; so, I did have to directly contact a few more players individually in order to ensure good representation of all leagues and divisions.

This ended up being a somewhat time consuming task, but I hope that this section of the book is accurate and interesting for all readers.

I know that there are literally hundreds of other softball players who could have been featured in the book. I can name several dozen right off the top of my head. But at some point I had to quit gathering more names and put this book together. After all, I just wanted to present the reader with a representative cross-section of players.

And all of this process has occurred midst the corona virus crisis. The 2020 winter season ended early and the 2020 summer season started late, creating an uncertain period of about three months when there was no softball being played. Since I was not finished with collecting all of my information, things slowed down considerably for working on this book. But eventually by mid-June I was able to gather most of the information that I needed and to start work on writing and formatting the book. And now, here it is!

I sincerely hope:

- That newcomers will find the book informative enough to help them as they begin their journeys as softball players in The Villages® community.
- That other readers who have lived here awhile will also find the book interesting and helpful to understand what this softball fuss is all about.
- That veteran players and managers will learn something they didn't know about another league or about various players.

I look forward to reading (not writing) the next book about Villages softball that will fill in the gaps that I have left; and that it will feature interesting information on the next thousand players who move here to play this enjoyable game of senior softball.

Overall it has been a pleasure and my honor to be able to record just a small slice of what softball here is like. For that, I thank everyone who has contributed.

Men's Division One - Field of Honor Recipients

(L-R) John Wick (College Point, New York), Rick Connor (Long Island, NY), Bud Shelley (Long Island, New York), Rod Severson (Iowa), Tom Simmons (Michigan), Dick Kanyan (Pennsylvania), David Mamuscia (Auburn, NY & Woodhaven, MI)

Not shown: Ron Gustaitus (CT), Donnie Duell (NC), Dewey McVicker (OH), Jim Carter (MI), Dominick Formisano (NY)

New Recipients to be inducted in 2020: Doug Gerkin, Dave Sellars, Greg Foster, John Rebardo

Honor Roll (non- players): Lee Kochenour, Terry & Linda Yanny

*Wick, Duell, and McVicker are in the National Softball Hall of Fame

Photo courtesy of Dave Mamuscia (2019)

Ladies Travel Team – 'Golden Gals 70' – Photo taken in April 2019 at Valdosta, GA

Front Row (L-R): Midge Ferraro, Kathy Tittle, Sharon Baran, Patricia Sprouse, Carol Courter, Ruth Weil, Judy Cothran, Ronnie Rump, Karen Parrinello

Back Row (L-R): Tig Beatty, Ellie Bowers, Cindy Price, Barbara Lukens, Evelyn Beck, Beth Quesnel, Avis Vaught

Photo courtesy of Avis Vaught

Central Florida League Champs –

Team Name – 'Softball's-R-Game'
Summer 2017 Season

Standing (L-R) - John Kushner, Tom Bortle, Bob Roth, Dan Kincaid, Jack Meagher, Rocky Spottswood, Bill Naasz

Kneeling (L-R) - Jim Crabtree, Charlie Clare, Bill Nesbit, Gary Nicolay, Co-Mgr. Ed Krisha

Absent - Jack Marx Co-Mgr., Dennis Bauch, Fred Weingard

Softball's R Game won both the regular season and the tournament championships.

Photo courtesy of Gary Nicolay and Ed Krisha.

Knudson Field

From RCF looking toward home plate.

Top – Scorer's Booth behind the screen with a view of the batter's box (L) and the home plate (R) where runners score. Bottom – Knudson's RF foul pole and 228' fence.

Saddlebrook

Walkway between fields, looking toward the score tower.

Top – Humorous sign at concession area.
Bottom – Concession stand and seating area.

Buffalo Glen

Centrally located scorer's tower overlooking four fields.

Top – There are spacious parking lots at all fields.
Bottom – From the batting area looking toward the OF.

Soaring Eagle

Seating area between the two fields at Soaring Eagle.

Top – From score tower looking out over field two.
Bottom – From beyond the RCF fence looking toward
field one with the score tower in the background.

Everglades

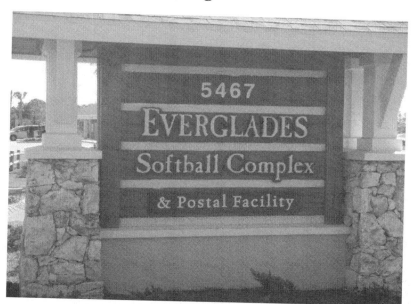

Walkway from the parking lot to the fields and dugouts.

Top – Typical electronic scoreboard at all softball fields.
Bottom – 300' fences and 15' warning track at Everglades,
Soaring Eagle, Buffalo Glen, and Saddlebrook.

Top – Glass case information boards at all locations.
Bottom – Pre-game warm-up areas between fields at all
locations.

Top – Pitcher's screen, batter's box, and scoring plate (L)
Bottom – Nice dugouts at all fields.

Top – From LF warning track and foul line looking toward the playing field at Everglades.
Bottom – Flags flying at all fields.

Arena League

Off-Site Field

Sacks Field in Lady Lake

Near The Villages

Top – Fence is 250' at Sacks Field.
Bottom – Scorer's box at Sacks Field.

REFERENCES

- ***20th Anniversary Ladies Softball Celebration Booklet*** provided to the author by Judy Wanko.

-Various websites for senior softball and softball in The Villages® community.

- Conversations with, and information supplied by: Pam Henry, Danny Jacobs, Andrew Esposito, Victoria Blackstock, Avis Vaught, Billy and Jeri Taylor, Matt Spanier, Darlene Hedrick, Jack Kleffman, Ted Ramirez, Joe Rocco, Terry Cole, Judy Wanko, Bob Hrabak, Bob Nyce, Wayne Lockman, Pam Napoletano, Wally Dias, Ron Lottes, John Raines, Bob Baker, Frenchie Le Tan, Gloria Tallee Miller, Tom McGann, Jack Nagle, Vernon Brooks, Jan Washburn, Jack Marx, Cathy Norris, Joe Sanchez, Karen Coll, Billy Layton, Charlie Monton, Jane Girotti, Wayne Meyer, Bill DiCarlo, Marie Panza, Dick Kanyan, Dave Bigelow, Dave Mamuscia, and others mentioned at various places in the book.

- Special thanks to all of those who provided their Bio Sheets to be included in the Appendix of this book. Those provided a personal touch that will give readers a glimpse into the lives of the individuals who make softball in The Villages® Community such a wonderful activity.

OTHER BOOKS BY DAN KINCAID

The Penicillin Kids, the 1966 West Virginia Class AA State Basketball Champions, 2015.

Your.....Wayne National Forest, Vol.I, a historical collection of the author's weekly Ohio newspaper columns from 1981 and 1982, 2016.

Your.....Chattahoochee National Forest, a historical collection of the author's weekly Georgia newspaper columns from December 1978 – June 1980, 2016.

Kade Holley, Forest Ranger, Vol.I, fictional accounts of Kade's adventures on National Forests in Minnesota, Ohio, North Carolina, and Washington, 2017.

Your.....Wayne National Forest, Vol.II, a historical collection of the author's weekly Ohio newspaper columns from 1983-1986, 2017.

Your.....Wayne National Forest, Vol.III, a historical collection of the author's weekly Ohio newspaper columns from 1987-1990, 2018.

Kade Holley, Forest Ranger, Vol.II, fictional accounts of Kade's adventures on National Forests in Georgia, West Virginia, Minnesota, Ohio, and Colorado, 2018.

A Gift to the Nation-From Ohio and Wayne National Forest, the 1987 Capitol Christmas Tree, 2019.

Kade Holley, Forest Ranger, Vol.III, fictional accounts of Kade's adventures on National Forests in West Virginia, Georgia, Ohio, and Minnesota, 2019.

West Virginia Romances: Tales of Young Love in the Mountain State, 2020.

All books are available at Amazon.com, Booksamillion.com, and Barnesandnoble.com. There is more information about the author and his books on the website: https://dankincaid.com

AUTHOR BIO – DAN KINCAID

The author, a West Virginia native, embarks on covering one of Florida's most popular outdoor sports in his 11th book: <u>Softball in The Villages® Community.</u>

His first book covered his high school's 1966 state basketball championship in Huntington, WV. Eight of his books revolve around experiences during a 31-year career with the U.S. Forest Service at National Forest locations in West Virginia, Ohio, Minnesota, Georgia, and North Carolina, as well as temporary details, training and various other assignments in Colorado, Kentucky, California, Indiana, Washington, Michigan, Montana, and Tennessee. In addition, he spent several years with state forestry agencies in West Virginia and Ohio, as well as in private sector forestry in Kentucky, Illinois, Missouri, and Tennessee.

Kincaid's most recent previous book, his 10th, was published in April 2020 and is a collection of teenage/young adult romance stories.

Kincaid received a Bachelor of Science degree in Forest Resource Management from West Virginia University; a Masters degree in Forestry/Environmental Management from Duke University; and a Teaching Certification for Biology and General Science from Marietta College in Ohio.

Dan and his wife, Vicki, are currently retired and living in Florida, where they enjoy the winter weather. He plays softball and contemplates writing his next book - number 12.

Made in the USA
Columbia, SC
06 August 2020